Furniture
Upholstery

By the Editors of
Sunset Books and
Sunset Magazine

Lane Publishing Co.
Menlo Park, California

Supervising Editor
DENISE VAN LEAR

Research & Text
MICHAEL SCOFIELD
SUDHA IRWIN

Editorial Consultant
HOLLY LYMAN ANTOLINI

Technical Consultants
ART BONNER
SAL FRENDO

Design
CYNTHIA HANSON

Photography
STEVE W. MARLEY

Illustrations
MARY KNOWLES

Cover
Photographed by
JACK MCDOWELL

Acknowledgments

It takes the time and cooperation of many people to create a book like this. In addition to the designers whose names appear in the photo captions, we wish to thank the following individuals, places, and organizations for their assistance: Abbey's Upholstery Shop, A. G. Furniture Refinishing and Repair, David Arrow Interiors, the staff of Art-Tistic Interiors, Bix Furniture Service, Blenwell Upholsterers, Grace Brown, Busvan Storage Company, Delaney Brothers Interiors, J & G Upholstery, Jim Pearson, and Tri J Fabrics. Special thanks go to Linda J. Selden for her research in furniture frame repair, to Diane Tapscott for assisting with photography, and to Richard Sachs, Ells Marugg, Joe Seney, and Elizabeth Hall for art preparation. We also express appreciation to the numerous charitable organizations whose decorator showcases served as inspiration for the color photographs that appear in this book.

Editor, Sunset Books: David E. Clark

CONTENTS

Getting Started

Whatever prompted you to open this book—the needlepoint cover disintegrating on Grandma's attic heirloom, a spring suddenly coiling out of the couch in the den, the tattered wing chair you bought at the flea market Sunday—whatever the problem is, relax. Soon you'll have that piece of furniture looking like new. You'll find that the craft of reupholstering not only is fun to learn, but it allows you to recondition old furniture at a fraction of the cost you'd pay for it new. By following the instructions in this book, and allowing plenty of time, you'll discover you can produce eye-pleasing work on your first try.

This is primarily a book for beginners, concentrating on the simpler types of upholstered furniture. You'll note that many of the drawings in the how-to-do-it chapters of the book portray a fully upholstered armchair. It is featured in the explicit step-by-step instructions because the techniques used on it are basic for many other kinds of furniture as well.

Five other basic types of furniture—a fully upholstered wing chair, an open-arm chair, an attached-cushion ottoman, a fully upholstered barrel-back chair, and a chair with a pad seat—are also described in the book. They require some specially adapted reupholstering techniques in addition to the basic ones given for the fully upholstered armchair. You'll find

these special techniques detailed, when necessary, in the text and drawings.

Upholstered furniture, however, varies in style almost as much as people vary in looks. If your furniture differs a great deal from the examples in this book, you may still be able to adapt the techniques given in the following chapters to your reupholstering project. However, you *may* find you need further assistance from experts in coping with your furniture's unique or complex characteristics.

The more difficult your piece is to reupholster, the more likely you are to need expert instruction. For example, if you plan to reupholster with vinyl or leather, or if your furniture sports channels (stuffed tubes of fabric, creating a vertical ribbed effect) or tufts (fabric pleated into indentations, held with buttons), you may need sophisticated skills requiring experience and personal assistance. Such style variations are too complex to be covered in this book.

If you decide to take on the challenge of your piece's idiosyncrasies, you can get the assistance you need in a number of ways. Check with your local professional upholsterers (see "Upholsterers" in the Yellow Pages) to see if a friendly one is willing to offer you advice or let you observe his or her work. Or phone your local community college or high school district (see "Schools—Secondary & Elementary" and "Schools—Universities & Colleges" in the Yellow Pages) for adult education courses.

Keep it simple if you can

Most upholstered furniture doesn't require stripping to the bare frame before you reupholster it; the chances are you only need to remove the old outer-cover fabric and top layer of cotton padding before replacing them with new, leaving the original stuffing, springs, and webbing alone.

The following tests indicate how much dismantling you'll probably have to do. Remove all the loose cushions first.

• Run your palm over the furniture's seat and inside back. Is the surface smooth? Does it bounce back when you depress it? "No" to either question means you may have to replace or recondition the old stuffing, and perhaps reanchor or replace the springs ("Furniture's Insides," pages 96–110, gives details).

• Turn the furniture over. If the bottom is covered with a black or tan fabric (called a "dustcatcher"), pull a corner off the bottom of the frame. Look for

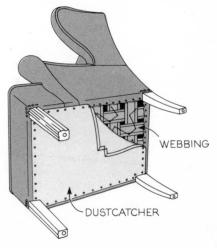

WEBBING

DUSTCATCHER

crisscrossed webbing. Does it sag? Does it appear to have been worn through in places? "Yes" to either question means you should reinforce it with new webbing (see page 97).

Some older furniture sports metal strips in place of webbing. Unless the metal has snapped, making the springs sag, you will not have to reinforce or replace the strips with new webbing.

When appraising how much work and expense a reupholstering project requires, you can apply other rules of thumb. For example, the smaller the piece of furniture, the less fabric you will have to buy. The fewer fabric-covered curves your furniture has, the easier reupholstering it becomes.

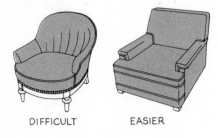

DIFFICULT   EASIER

Test your furniture's construction quality by trying to wiggle the back and arms. The more they move, the more bracing and gluing you'll need to have done (see "Furniture Repair," page 32).

Testing furniture's toughness

Furniture that was built to last is the kind you'll probably want to reupholster, no matter how tattered or wobbly it is when you find it. If you're combing the attic or shopping at antique or used furniture stores and garage sales, you can test durability in two ways.

• Lift similar pieces. The heavier ones are built of alder, mahogany, oak, or maple, and will endure far longer than lighter

pieces built of fir, pine, or pressed wood.

• Look underneath. Are staples and metal braces now holding the piece together? Let someone else have it. Furniture held together by dowels, wood braces, and screws, even though loose, may be worth repairing (see page 32).

Where to find tools & supplies

Like woodworking, upholstering is a craft to which you can bring a seemingly endless variety of tools, gadgets, and materials. Yet with a few tools—some of which you may already have—and a dozen supplies, you can complete most jobs satisfactorily.

You have three sources from which to purchase kits or individual items of upholstering equipment. An increasing number of "Fabric Shops" (the term often used in the Yellow Pages) stock not only fabric but padding, foam, upholsterer's skewers, and essential tools. Under "Upholsterers' Supplies" in the Yellow Pages, you'll find retail stores specializing in foam; these stores usually carry upholstering tools as well. You'll also see listings for upholstery wholesalers, who sometimes sell to the do-it-yourselfer. Rather than asking about supplies over the phone, it's best to visit these busy wholesalers in person to maximize your chances of picking up a hard-to-find item.

Often the easiest place to buy supplies like webbing, springs, and edge rolls is a professional upholsterer's shop. A professional upholsterer will also sell you fabric, and may even be willing to perform tough sewing tasks for you on an industrial-grade machine, for a fee.

Tools of the trade

The following is an alphabetical listing of the tools you'll need for most reupholstering projects.

Claw tool. The bent shank and beveled, forked blade of the claw tool are especially designed to rid furniture quickly of old staples, tacks, and fabric. If you can't locate a claw tool, use an inexpensive wood chisel, an upholsterer's ripping tool (bent shank, chisel-shaped head), or a screwdriver.

Cutting table. A smooth 4 by 8-foot sheet of ½ to 1-inch-thick plywood, perched waist-high, eases the laying out and cutting of fabric sections.

Electric stapler. Applying staples instead of tacks to the outer cover is faster and tends to hold fabric more evenly. Be forewarned, though, that staples, once driven into wood, are difficult to pry free.

Magnetized tack hammer. One end of this hammer's special head picks up and holds tacks while planting them; the other end drives them in. Unless you own a mallet, you can use the side of the tack hammer's head on the claw tool's butt to remove old fabric, tacks, and staples.

Needles. A curved 3-inch needle eases such fabric sewing chores as attaching the outside-back outer-cover fabric section to the outside arms (page 78). Use a curved 6-inch needle for sewing on edge rolls (page 108) and stitching burlap to springs. A straight 12 to 18-inch needle speeds the anchoring of spring bottoms to webbing (page 100). A double-pointed straight needle is even easier to use; you may be able to find one at an upholstery supply shop.

Be sure your needle has a round point; triangular-pointed needles are designed to penetrate leathers and vinyls (materials not recommended for beginners).

Pliers. For pulling a broken tack or staple free, or ripping out old fabric and padding, nothing does

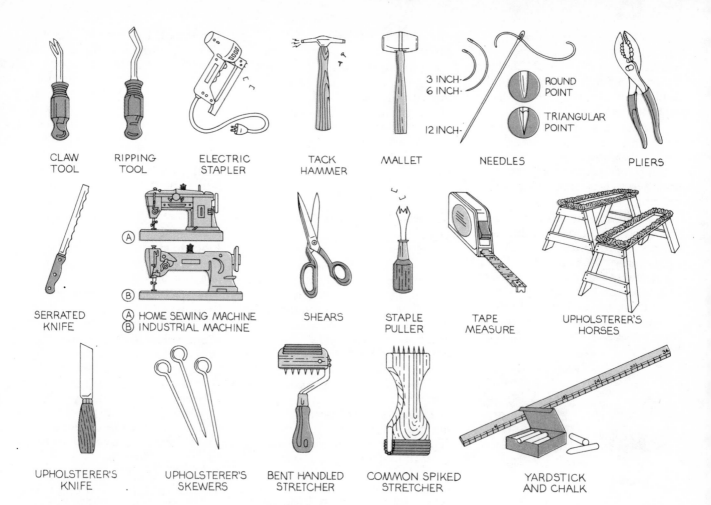

CLAW TOOL

RIPPING TOOL

ELECTRIC STAPLER

TACK HAMMER

MALLET

3 INCH
6 INCH
12 INCH

ROUND POINT

TRIANGULAR POINT

NEEDLES

PLIERS

SERRATED KNIFE

Ⓐ HOME SEWING MACHINE
Ⓑ INDUSTRIAL MACHINE

SHEARS

STAPLE PULLER

TAPE MEASURE

UPHOLSTERER'S HORSES

UPHOLSTERER'S KNIFE

UPHOLSTERER'S SKEWERS

BENT HANDLED STRETCHER

COMMON SPIKED STRETCHER

YARDSTICK AND CHALK

the job as fast as an ordinary pair of pliers. You'll also find pliers handy for replacing zigzag springs.

Serrated knife. To shape polyurethane foam for restuffing a seat, back, or cushion (page 90), a long bread or carving knife works fine; an electric carving knife is ideal. You can even make do with a small saw.

Sewing machine. A sewing machine speeds many chores. Use it to sew darts, welt (fabric-wrapped seam trim), zippers, skirts, and cushions; to join major sections of fabric; and to attach scraps called "pull-throughs" or "stretchers" to the fabric cover.

(Stretchers are used to extend the cover fabric down to the frame in hidden parts of the furniture.)

For light and medium-weight fabrics, a portable or cabinet model machine will do; use a #16 or #100 needle. The zipper foot that comes with most machines aids in creating welt and attaching it to different fabric sections.

For heavy fabrics such as tapestry, corduroy, and damask, use a #18 or #110 needle. Sewing through three to five layers of these fabrics can cause motor-heating problems with home machines. Perhaps you can find a friendly professional who, for a fee, will sew your heavy fabric on an industrial-grade machine. Or if cost doesn't deter you, rent a machine yourself. (Look under "Sewing Machines—Industrial" in the Yellow Pages.)

Shears. A pair of shears with blades at least 5 inches long works best; the longer the blades,

the fewer cuts you have to make. Upholsterer's shears with one bent shank allow the fabric to lie flat while you cut. Also use shears for severing old twine, shaping rubberized-hair stuffing, and paring chalk tips to a fine point.

Staple puller. A luxury, this stub-handled tool is designed to rout staples from wood faster and more easily than a claw tool or chisel.

Tape measure. A spring-return, 12-foot-long steel tape measure assures easy estimates of how much new fabric you'll need. A cloth tape is less handy: it tends to twist, and you have to pin its free end down when spanning distances longer than your outstretched arms.

Upholsterer's horses. These padded, trough-topped trestles raise furniture off the floor, so you don't get a sore back from bending over to work. Directions for making upholsterer's horses appear on page 62.

Upholsterer's knife. This tool is designed to cut away waste fabric, once a section is tacked into position. You can substitute a retractable utility knife, a razor blade, or even a well-honed paring knife.

Upholsterer's skewers. These 3 to 4-inch-long pins serve two purposes: they hold new covers in place while you shape fabric and can be used as picks to redistribute padding under sewn or tacked-down covers. (Caution: skewers will leave marks on tightly woven fabrics.)

Webbing stretcher. You'll need this tool only if your furniture sports sagging webbing.

Yardstick and chalk. With a yardstick, you can chalk accurate fabric-section guidelines. (Test the yardstick for straightness by setting it on edge along a tabletop.) Sharpened blackboard chalk draws lines that are easier to see and easier to brush out than tailor's chalk or pencil lines.

Upholstering supplies

Below is an alphabetical listing of supplies you may need for your reupholstering project.

Burlap. This fabric covers webbing or springs to provide a smooth base for stuffing, and restrains bits of stuffing from drifting through the outer cover. Used under the cover on outside backs and arms, it buffers the fabric against pokes.

Cord, twine, and thread. Buy 5/32-inch-thick unwaxed jute cord to form welt. Waxed jute, 3/32 inch thick, is called "spring twine." You use it to reyoke coil springs together and secure them to the

frame. Use upholsterer's twine, or heavy-duty polyester thread, to secure stuffing to burlap, attach burlap, and hand-sew the outer cover.

Edge roll. Also called "fox edging," this thick cord, wrapped in burlap, keeps the frame from abrading fabric and creates a dike to contain stuffing.

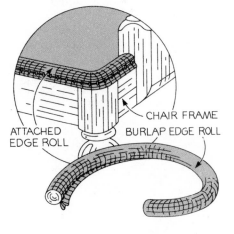

ATTACHED EDGE ROLL

CHAIR FRAME

BURLAP EDGE ROLL

Edgewire. The seats and backs with the most bounce are those whose springs extend to the frame's outer edges. A stiff wire, to which the outer springs are tied, lines these edges. This wire is known as "edgewire." You can leave the old edgewire intact, just as you can the springs themselves.

EDGEWIRE

Fabrics. You'll want three types of fabric: one for the dustcatcher, one for decking, and one for the outer cover. Secured beneath

your furniture to keep stuffing particles from dropping free, the dustcatcher is usually a fine-woven cotton called "cambric." Use muslin or denim decking on your furniture's deck (the cushion-supporting platform that will be hidden by loose seat cushions). You'll read about the third type of fabric, your furniture's outer cover, in the next chapter.

DECKING

Gimp. This flat, ornamental braid hides tacks and outer-cover edges on exposed wood. Use polyvinyl acetate—called "white" glue—to hold gimp in place.

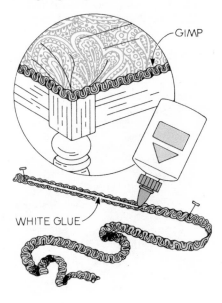

GIMP

WHITE GLUE

Jute webbing. Interwoven 3½-inch-wide strips of jute webbing provide a foundation for most upholstered seats, backs, arms, and wings in older furniture. Only zigzag-sprung furniture, and wood, rubber, or metal foundations do not require jute webbing.

JUTE WEBBING

Loose hog or horse hair stuffing. You probably can't find this stuffing new, but you can usually reuse whatever your furniture contains.

Moss stuffing. Slightly less resilient than hair, moss is nearly as durable. Try to reuse whatever moss your furniture contains.

Padding. Inch-thick felted cotton pads the outer fabric cover, softening its feel.

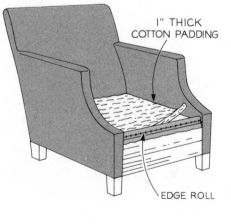

1" THICK COTTON PADDING

EDGE ROLL

Polyurethane foam. More and more frequently used in place of springs in cushions, and in place of loose or rubberized hair in seats and backs, foam is designated according to density—soft, medium, and firm.

Rubberized-hair stuffing. Stuffing of this material lasts longer than polyurethane foam but is more expensive and difficult to find. The hog or horse hair is held together by synthetic-fiber netting. Rubber coating preserves the hair's resilience.

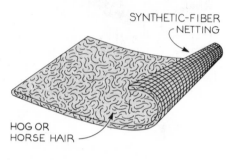

SYNTHETIC-FIBER NETTING

HOG OR HORSE HAIR

Springs. The larger your chair or sofa, the more likely it is to boast springs, especially in the seat and back. Coil springs are most common in pre-1960 furniture; zigzag (also called "no-sag") springs appear in post-1960 furniture.

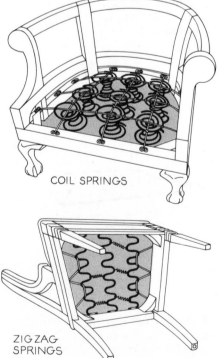

COIL SPRINGS

ZIG ZAG SPRINGS

Tacking strips. These ½-inch-wide strips of cardboard give straight edges to your outer cover. Buy them in rolls from an upholstery shop, or buy sheet cardboard from an art supply store and cut it into strips yourself.

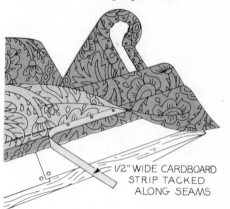

1/2" WIDE CARDBOARD STRIP TACKED ALONG SEAMS

Tacks. The tips of upholstering tacks are hair-fine; even an initial light tap keeps them upright. If you need to replace only the outer cover and outer layer of padding, use #3 tacks (3/8 inch long). For delicate operations, such as attaching fabric to front arm panels, use #2 tacks (2/8 inch long). You'll need #10 or #12 tacks (5/8 or 6/8 inch long) to fasten spring twine to most frames, though #8 tacks (9/16 inch long) are needed to fasten twine to hardwood and antique frames.

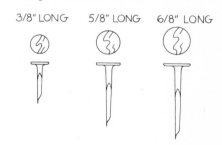

3/8" LONG   5/8" LONG   6/8" LONG

Zippers. You'll want a zipper for the back of each loose cushion. At a fabric shop, buy the lengths you need off a roll, or buy precut zippers.

A Gallery of
Decorating Ideas

Part of the fun of any reupholstering project is to visualize how various fabric colors and patterns would look on your furniture.

Here we present an array of fabric choices, displayed on furniture ranging from the simplest of reupholstering tasks—the pad-seated desk or dining chair—to the more ambitious undertakings: wing and armchairs, love seats, and sofas. Pay special attention to attractive detail-work, such as the use of contrasting welt (page 24) and buttons (page 12). Such imaginative touches give character and flair to your furniture's finished appearance.

On the following pages, you'll see how a single revitalized sofa or chair can revamp the entire decorating theme of a room. Such a transformation could inspire you to purchase extra fabric for matching draperies and other accessories. It could even entice you to move on to more elaborate reupholstering projects.

The new and the antique merge in a matching French antique chair and ottoman. Contemporary confetti-striped fabric enlivens and positively flirts with the dark carved wood frame. Design: The Homestead.

Elegant Beginnings

Satin makes magic on a pad-seated chair. High-gloss wood, fabric, and Bukhara-style carpet are perfectly coordinated—the result of imaginative decorating. Design: Ron Newman.

Graceful accompaniment: Fabric's diminutive pattern adapts well to a delicate antique such as this romantic piano seat à deux. Design: Glenna Cook.

Dramatic contrast results from the matching of an airy floral fabric with rich old wood. Double welting gives authority to small, delicate furniture pieces. Design: The Homestead.

Minimal upholstering makes pad seats very approachable for novices. Here, a simple antique side chair was easily adorned in a flame-pattern bargello fabric. Design: Glenna Cook.

Wing Chairs

Regal, yet comfortable in any setting, a hand-woven fabric covers a well-stuffed wing chair and ottoman. Design: Glenna Cook.

Inviting as a woolly blanket on a cold winter's night, this wing chair glories in a vivid Scottish plaid. Popular as they are, plaids require careful matching for a professional appearance. Design: Sharron Bishop.

Country charm of a French provincial wing chair and its round footstool is enhanced by a subdued cream and rust fabric. Buttons add personality to the inside back and cushion. Design: Britt M. Chappell.

Alluring twins are reupholstered identically in a pleasant yellow print. Rolled arms, tailored skirts, and T-shaped cushions are standard details of many reupholstery projects. Design: Christy Neidig/Vintage Properties.

Dining Chairs

Chairs take the spotlight in an understated dining room. Smart brass tacks secure lively wool fabric to antique wood seats and backs. Design: Los Gatos Porch.

Zing of contrasting color transforms the simplest chairs into a decorator's dream, with imaginatively styled fabric. Here, plainly upholstered pad seats are perked up by knife-edge cushions with contrasting welt and leg bows. Design: Jean Crawford.

Curvaceous welt outlines interesting frame shape of dining chairs, picking up the red in the rich brocade fabric. Brilliant blue walls and a red and blue Iranian Kilim rug complete the room's color harmony.

Sofas & Love Seats

Stripes in sunny yellow span a traditional, rolled-arm sofa. Brightly printed throw pillows create a cheerful, casual feeling. Design: Christy Neidig/ Vintage Properties.

Lavish crewel design is a splendid choice for a simple sofa in a room full of antique furniture and brass. Gently turned draperies and sash repeat the sofa's upholstery fabric. Design: Glenna Cook.

Mellow green gingham makes an eye-soothing cover for this cushy love seat, while complementing the bone hue of the carpeting and curtains. Design: Glenna Cook.

Antiques

A potpourri of prints lends whimsy to a gracious, old-fashioned armchair. Star-shaped design in decorative sashes and throw pillow adds boldness. Design: Delsa Ham.

V.I.P. treatment is demanded by rare antiques. Nothing less than a textured blue satin could complement the lustrous carved wood frame of this old armchair. Wickerlike "monk's weave" back peeks from behind a knife-edge cushion. Design: Domicile.

Straight up the walls runs the same fabric used on a reupholstered Victorian day bed, intensifying the exquisite lines of the bed's dark wood. Design: Christy Neidig/ Vintage Properties.

Dainty Victorian curves of armchair are accentuated by subtly striped cream and white upholstery fabric. Throw pillow's blue accents pick up design of fanciful, woven rug. Design: Glenna Cook.

The Contemporary Look

In a play of textures, tawny tweed is matched to sleek brass chairs, perfectly in keeping with the rugged feeling of this room. A handcrafted wool carpet adds another nubbly texture variation. Design: Cole-Wheatman Interior Designers, Inc.

Tree-branch inspired, these dining chair frames receive the luxury of printed fawn-colored suede. Working with suede calls for advanced skills, and its thickness may require you to use an industrial-grade machine to sew the double welt trim shown here. Design: Bob Rogers.

Updating a classic rolled-arm sofa,
this quilted cover has an undulating
wave pattern. Weltless, skirtless—
even the sofa's front arm panels were
abandoned for modern simplicity and
sleekness. Design: Carla Condon.

Upholstered Groupings

Ever-reliable mix of fabrics: choose a quiet solid color from among the colors in a print and use it as background throughout the room. Here, white sofa, carpeting, and draperies offer a tasteful backdrop for blue and white floral print on chairs. Design: Dick and Marianne Andrews.

A sweep of blue sofas complements the nautical mood of an easy-going room. Special features: loose back and arm cushions for extra comfort. Design: Christy Neidig/ Vintage Properties.

A trio in apricot: Matched chairs and ottoman spice a genteel guest room. Tautly covered, even over tapering legs, the ensemble bespeaks elegance. Design: Miriam Bumburger and Shirley White.

...Groupings

Brightly rimmed armchairs, upholstered in sturdy navy velvet, are edged in red welt to tie in with love seat's red cover. The grouping as a whole blends with Oriental rugs, Imari plates, blue walls.

Classical couch and armchair share an equally classical covering. Floral sprays on fabric are carefully matched at seams for continuous motif flow. Design: Corinne Wiley.

Working with Fabric

No matter how much work you put into fixing up a chair's or sofa's insides, it's the appearance of the outer cover that will be your most notable mark of success. This chapter helps you choose the best fabric for your furniture, and then shows you how to estimate and measure the amount of fabric you'll need. Instructions for measuring, shaping, and sewing the fabric begin on page 33.

Selecting fabric

Faced with today's proliferation of prints, manmade fibers, and fiber blends, you may feel slightly overwhelmed when trying to choose the best fabric for your project. But don't despair: the following tips will help simplify the decision.

How to pick colors

A feeling of harmony is your main object in selecting colors for a room. This means that the colors of the fabric you choose for your new upholstery should complement those already established in your room's walls, draperies, rugs, and furniture. The following are some guidelines to use in your color selection.

• Neutral or earth-tone colors blend into almost any surroundings.

• Many bright colors can be lively, but may also give your piece more prominence than you wish—particularly if it is a large one, such as a sofa.

• To add a cheerful note to your room, introduce pinks, oranges, reds, or yellows. To subdue your color scheme, use blues, browns, or tans.

• Remember that any color placed against a dark background appears lighter than it is. The same color will look darker when placed against a light background. Grouping light colors on one side of a room and dark colors on the other will destroy the room's color balance.

Patterns or solids?

A geometric or floral print can perk up plain surroundings, but if a room's wallpaper, draperies, rug, or other furniture already boasts one pattern, adding a second may cause visual confusion. One rule of thumb is, the smaller the room, the fewer different patterns it should contain. Also, large patterns tend to overpower small rooms and small pieces of furniture.

The larger your room is, the larger your furniture should look, to achieve a sense of proportion. Stripes can make a piece of furniture look wider than it really is, if laid along it horizontally. Placed vertically, stripes make furniture look more compact.

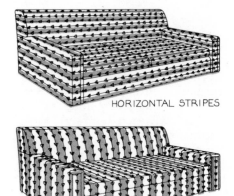

HORIZONTAL STRIPES

VERTICAL STRIPES

If you're inclined to choose a print, bear in mind that some prints can cause centering or matching problems. When the time comes to cut your fabric and assemble the outer-cover sections, you'll find that swirls, geometrics, and uniform colors are easiest to piece together, because you needn't line up their designs. Florals add difficulty—and fabric waste—because you have to center the design on the furniture's inside and outside back, inside and outside arms, and on both sides of the cushion. Stripes must be lined up on all planes of the furniture. Most difficult of all are the plaids and checks: you have to match the columns and rows in both directions at every seam.

A sure way to discover if a fabric requires matching is this: in the store, unroll enough yardage to lay two sections of fabric side by side, selvages (borders) aligned so that the pattern continues across the two widths as if they were one. Now shift one section slightly—if the pattern fluctuates jarringly, the fabric will have to be matched.

Don't buy patterned fabric if the pattern is printed severely off-grain (if it doesn't run parallel to the side-to-side threads), because you'll never be able to align the pattern properly on your furniture.

Questions to ask yourself

When shopping for upholstering fabrics, you'll want answers to the following questions:

1. Will my sewing machine stitch through five layers of this fabric, when I begin to garnish the cushions with welt. You may have to turn the machine wheel by hand, or pay to have a professional upholsterer do the sewing, to avoid overheating your machine. When in doubt, buy ¼ yard of the fabric and test it on your machine.

2. Is the fabric backed? When you turn some fabrics over, especially those woven from manmade fibers, you see what appears to be a dried white paste spread across the back. Called "backing," the substance is latex, used to keep threads from pulling free. The thicker the backing, the less expensive the fabric (because fewer threads are used per square inch). Don't select a fabric with heavy backing; it will be stiff and difficult to work with.

3. Will the fabric wear well? Long wear depends more on a weave's tightness—the number of threads per square inch of fabric—than on the type of fiber in the weave. The tighter the weave, the less the fabric stretches. You can test tightness by trying to stretch the fabric along the selvage (not on the bias). If you remain uncertain, try to look through the fabric—the less light you see, the denser the fabric is, and the tighter the weave.

STRETCH ALONG SELVAGE

4. Are the colors likely to fade? The words "Vat Dyed" or "Vat Colors" imprinted along the selvage of a fabric indicate that the dyes won't dissolve in water.

All dyes fade somewhat, but dark-colored fabrics will show more fading, and show it sooner, than light-colored ones. All fabrics fade badly if exposed to long periods of direct sunlight.

5. Does the fabric stretch? All fabric stretches to some degree, especially on the bias. But the more it stretches, the more likely it will be to lose its shape eventually, even though tacked down.

6. How often must I clean the fabric? The lighter the color and the plainer the fabric, the more readily you'll see grime accumulate. Manmade fibers repel soiling better than natural ones, but natural fibers clean better, once soiled. Fabrics marked "soil-resistant," or the equivalent, are the most carefree.

7. Which way does the design run? On many pieces of furniture you can save fabric by using the technique called "railroading" (see page 28). You can railroad the majority of fabrics on the market.

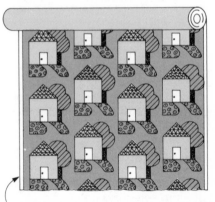

SOME PATTERNS SHOULD NOT BE RAILROADED

Some fabrics, however, don't adapt well to this technique. For example, prints showing people, animals, buildings, trees, and flowers with stems look strange when turned sideways, as required for railroading. Also, velvets and corduroys don't railroad

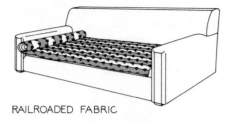

RAILROADED FABRIC

VERTICALLY RUN FABRIC

well because they have pile—tiny, stand-up threads that tend to lean in one direction. Directing the pile toward the furniture's left or right arm, rather than down, changes the color effect. You may also not want to turn striped fabrics sideways, since their visual thrust from side to side will make your furniture look lower and wider than it actually is.

8. Is the fabric in keeping with the style of furniture you plan to upholster? Bold stripes, for instance, may overpower a delicate chair. On the other hand, a dainty design might look odd on a large, masculine-looking sofa.

Where to buy fabrics

Home furnishings stores sometimes sell fabrics, but your best bet is to look in the Yellow Pages under "Fabric Shops." These outlets sell textiles in great variety, both the traditional heavy upholstery fabrics and the newer, lighter weight, "decorator" fabrics, as well as some supplies with which to fashion them into finished goods.

Professional upholsterers will sell you fabrics, too. They keep a supply of sample books with swatches that range from 6 to 18-inch squares. You make your selection there at the upholsterer's; usually you can't take the samples home.

UPHOLSTERERS' SAMPLE BOOKS

Probably the best sources of distinctive fabrics are interior decorators and designers. These specialists have access to high-quality fabrics that you can't find elsewhere, and they will bring samples to your home. Theirs is a service, of course, for which you must expect to pay.

Regardless of where you purchase your fabric, be sure to examine *all* the material carefully, checking for correct pattern, color, and fabric width, and for any flaws and misweaves. Returns or trades are rarely allowed once you begin to cut the fabric.

It's always wise to purchase more fabric than you expect to need—½ yard extra for a chair, 1 yard for a larger piece. Usually only the most experienced upholsterer can determine fabric needs with absolute precision, and the security of having a little leeway is well worth the extra cost, since fabric designs, like clothing styles, disappear fast. If you make a cutting mistake and wish to buy more fabric, your pattern may no longer be available.

When buying fabric, try to buy all of it off the same bolt. The same design's coloring may vary from bolt to bolt if the fabric was dyed at different times.

How to estimate yardage

The chart on pages 30–31 gives yardage estimates for 21 basic types of furniture. If your furniture differs from the types shown there, use the estimate given for the piece that most closely resembles your own. Or you can calculate precise yardage by measuring your piece (pages 40–45) and laying out its sections on a small-scale paper layout as described on pages 46–47.

In either case, if you choose a patterned fabric, see "Motif repeats" on page 28.

Padding requirements depend on the condition of your furniture. If you only need to replace or add the top layer of padding, plan on buying enough cotton padding to make up at least two-thirds of the amount estimated for the fabric cover in the "railroaded—no skirt" column of the Yardage Estimate Chart. Keep in mind that cotton padding usually is sold in 27-inch-wide lengths from a roll.

Whether you use the chart (which is faster) or do your own calculations, peruse the following definitions of terms to discover if you need to increase the basic yardage estimate to cover your furniture with your choice of fabric.

Skirt. The fabric panels that surround the base of a piece of furniture and drape to the floor are collectively called a "skirt." Often they improve the furniture's appearance by hiding marred or unsightly legs or by making the piece look less top-heavy.

To save fabric and make construction easier, we recommend a tailored skirt with a 1-inch hem and illusory pleats (see page 92). The chart gives yardage estimates which assume that all skirts are 6 inches long, and lined.

For the lining, buy sateen, lightweight duck or osnaburg—¾ yard for chairs, 1¼ yards for love

TAILORED SKIRT

seats and chaises, and 2 yards for sofas up to 96 inches wide. Both fabrics are made of heavy cotton fibers and are available in at least 48-inch widths.

Railroading vs. vertically run. To "railroad" means to align fabric horizontally, end to end along the width of a piece of furniture, and from front to back along its arms. On love seats and sofas, this method eliminates some seams on the outside and inside back, tight seat (no loose cushions), and the furniture's front (see illustration on page 27). Railroading often reduces the amount of fabric you need. It can save you approximately 10 percent on a skirtless, fully upholstered armchair, and 15 percent on a skirtless, 84-inch-wide sofa.

SKIRTLESS SOFA WITH RAILROADED FABRIC

Certain fabrics *must* be run vertically, however, with the fabric aligned from front to back over the furniture's height, and bottom to top over its arms. Page 26, Question 7, explains why.

Motif repeats. Some fabrics have prominent repeated designs—a building, a flower, a group of people—which you must center on various parts of your furniture in order to achieve a sense of balance. Other repeated patterns—stripes, checks, plaids, rows of small motifs—must be matched up as you fit the fabric pieces together. If the motifs of your fabric repeat every 3 inches, or more frequently, you needn't buy extra fabric to allow for centering or matching.

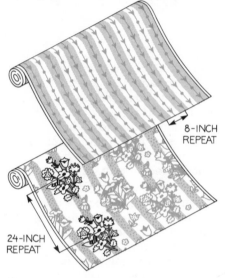

8-INCH REPEAT

24-INCH REPEAT

If your fabric's motifs repeat every 4 to 12 inches, add 8 inches per yard to your own calculations or the amount listed for your furniture in the Yardage Estimate Chart. If the motifs repeat every 13 to 20 inches, add 15 inches per yard to your own calculations or the chart estimate for your furniture. And if the motifs repeat every 21 to 28 inches, add 20 inches per yard to your own calculations or the amount estimated for your furniture in the chart.

Welt. The estimates in the Yardage Estimate Chart include an allowance for single welt, since welt may give your upholstering job the finished look it needs. Instructions on how to make welt begin on page 53.

You can also use contrasting fabric to make welt if you wish to highlight the seams. To make contrasting welt, buy contrasting fabric, allowing the same amounts you would for the single matching welt described above: 1 yard for chairs and chaises, 1¼ yards for love seats, 1¾ yards for sofas up to 84 inches wide, and 2¼ yards for sofas up to 96 inches wide.

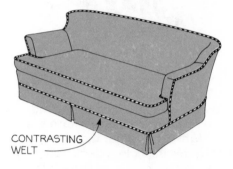

CONTRASTING WELT

If you wish to use double welt (see page 54), buy 1¾ yards of fabric for chairs and chaises, 2¾ yards for love seats, 3 yards for sofas up to 84 inches wide, and 3¾ yards for sofas up to 96 inches wide.

At a fabric store, pick up enough cord to make the welt. You can tell how much you'll need by measuring all the seams that show on your furniture. If you plan to attach a skirt, buy enough extra cord to encircle your furniture's circumference at skirt level. If you plan no skirt, the welt circling your furniture's base is optional, but don't forget to include enough cord to rim all the loose cushions. Be sure to double your measurements if you intend to make double welt.

Fabric widths. The chart estimates are based on traditional upholstery fabric's standard 54-inch width. Many fabrics, often lighter in weight but still suitable for upholstery, come in narrower widths. If the fabric you like is 50 inches wide, increase the chart, welt, and motif-repeat estimates by 10 percent; if it's 48 inches wide, increase all the estimates by 20 percent; if it's 45 inches wide, increase all the estimates by 30 percent.

If you're tempted to use 36-inch-wide fabric, increase the chart, welt, and motif-repeat estimates by 50 percent. But be warned: fabric narrower than 45 inches must often be pieced together, which means much more work for you.

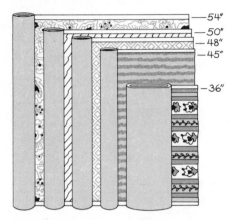

Decking. Many furniture types sport removable seat cushions; the fabric hidden beneath is called "decking," since it covers the furniture's deck. Instead of buying outer-cover fabric for the decking, you can save money by covering the deck with denim or medium-weight unbleached muslin.

DECKING

To determine how much decking to buy, measure your furniture's greatest width (usually along its front) and add 4 inches—2 inches for tacking on either side. Buy 36-inch-wide muslin, if you can; if not, 45-inch-wide material will do. Or ask a professional upholsterer to sell you special denim decking; most upholsterers store it on rolls for their own use.

Stretchers. Sewn to the bottom and side outer-cover edges of inside backs and some inside arms, and sometimes to the back edge of a tight seat, stretchers are fabric scraps, used to extend the outer cover in hidden areas of your furniture. They help reduce the amount of outer-cover fabric you need to buy, and thus reduce your costs. Cut them from the old outer cover, or from new-cover waste. After sewing the stretchers to the new outer cover, and pulling the cover tautly into position on your furniture, you'll tack or staple the stretchers to parts of the frame where they won't show.

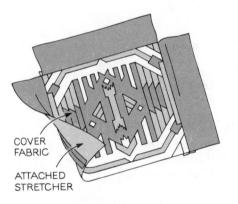

COVER FABRIC

ATTACHED STRETCHER

Dustcatcher. If a disintegrating old dustcatcher shields your furniture's bottom, you'll want to replace it with new fabric. Measure the old one to find out how much cambric or medium-weight unbleached muslin you'll need (see illustration on page 4).

The most popular upholstery fabrics

Fabrics for upholstering divide into two general categories and may even be displayed in different parts of the store. The traditional, heavier, so-called "upholstery" fabrics are woven to hold up under multitudes of sitters. "Decorator" fabrics or "dress goods" are lighter in weight, but often display bolder colors and greater pattern variety. Cotton constitutes the base for most of these lighter fabrics, because it's so easily printed.

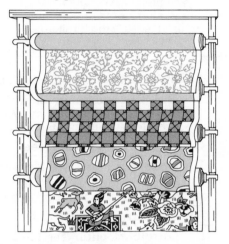

Though traditional upholstery fabrics wear longer than their lighter-weight brethren, they are so thick that your home machine may balk at stitching through five layers. Buy a swatch and test it, to be sure.

Many people confuse the word "fiber" with the word "fabric." The two are not interchangeable. Fibers, twisted into long strands called "yarns," are woven together to make fabrics.

You'll note as you shop that most fabrics are called by the fiber's common or brand name if that fiber comprises 100 percent of the weave. Thus the fabric called "linen" is woven of 100 percent linen fibers. The manmade "olefin" consists of 100 percent olefin fibers.

Other fabrics are named according to their fiber blends. The term "cotton/rayon" means a blend of those two fibers. "Cotton/polyester" usually consists of 35 percent cotton fiber and 65 percent polyester fiber.

YARDAGE ESTIMATE CHART

This chart is a guide to estimating the yardage needed to upholster certain basic types of furniture. The figures include allowances for single, noncontrasting welt. Tailored skirts are assumed to be 6 inches long and lined with a different fabric (see page 92).

If you prefer to calculate the precise yardage for your particular piece, first measure the furniture, following the directions on pages 33–48; then draw a paper layout, as directed, starting on page 34.

If motifs on your fabric are repeated less frequently than every 3 inches, add yardage as shown in "Motif repeats," page 28. If your fabric is less than 54 inches wide, see "Fabric widths" on page 28. Should you plan to add contrasting or double welt, see pages 53–54.

| | | Yardage: 54-inch-wide fabrics | | | |
| | | Railroaded | | Vertically run | |
		No skirt	Tailored skirt	No skirt	Tailored skirt
A	Standard ottoman (up to 22 by 22 inches)	1¾	2¾	2	3
B	Oversize ottoman with attached cushion (23 by 23 inches to 27 by 27 inches — see Measurement List, page 42)	2¼	3¾	2½	4
C	Chair with pad seat (see page 79)	2¼	3¾	2½	4
D	Open-arm chair (see Measurement List, page 43) *If you use double welt instead of gimp or braid, add ¾ yard to yardage estimate in each column.*	2¼	—	3	—
E	Open-arm cogswell	4¼	—	5	—
F	Barrelback chair (see Measurement List, page 43)	5¼	6¼	5½	6½
G	Platform rocker	5¼	6¾	5½	7
H	Fully upholstered armchair (see Measurement List, page 40)	5¼	6¾	6	7½
I	Armchair with removable back cushion	6¾	8¼	7½	9
J	Low-back wing chair	6¼	7¾	6½	8
K	High-back wing chair (see Measurement List, page 44)	6¼	8	6½	8¼
L	Chaise longue with no cushions	7½	9	7¾	9¾
M	Chaise longue with removable deck cushion	9	11	10¼	11¾
N	Chaise longue with removable deck & back cushions	10½	12½	11¾	13¼
O	Two-deck-cushion love seat (to 60 inches wide)	10	11½	11¼	12¾
P	Two-deck-cushion sofa (60 to 72 inches wide (73 to 84 inches wide) *Add 1 yard to yardage estimate in each column if width is same but cushions total three.*	12 13¾	14 15¾	13 15	15 17
Q	Two-deck-cushion wing sofa (60 to 72 inches wide) (73 to 84 inches wide) *Add 1 yard to yardage estimate in each column if width is same but cushions total three.*	12½ 14½	14½ 16½	13¾ 15¾	15¾ 17¾
R	Two-deck-cushion sofa (60 to 72 inches wide) with two removable back cushions Two-deck-cushion sofa (73 to 84 inches wide) with two removable back cushions *Add 2 yards to yardage estimate in each column if width is same but cushions total six.*	14 15¾	16 17¾	15 16½	17 18½
S	Three-deck-cushion sofa (96 inches wide)	14¾	16¾	16½	18
T	Three-deck-cushion wing sofa (96 inches wide)	15½	17½	17	19
U	Three-deck-cushion sofa (96 inches wide) with three removable back cushions	18¼	20¼	19	21

The following basic furniture styles are illustrated to help you estimate the amount of fabric you'll need. Your furniture may vary slightly: choose the illustration that most closely resembles the piece of furniture you plan to reupholster.

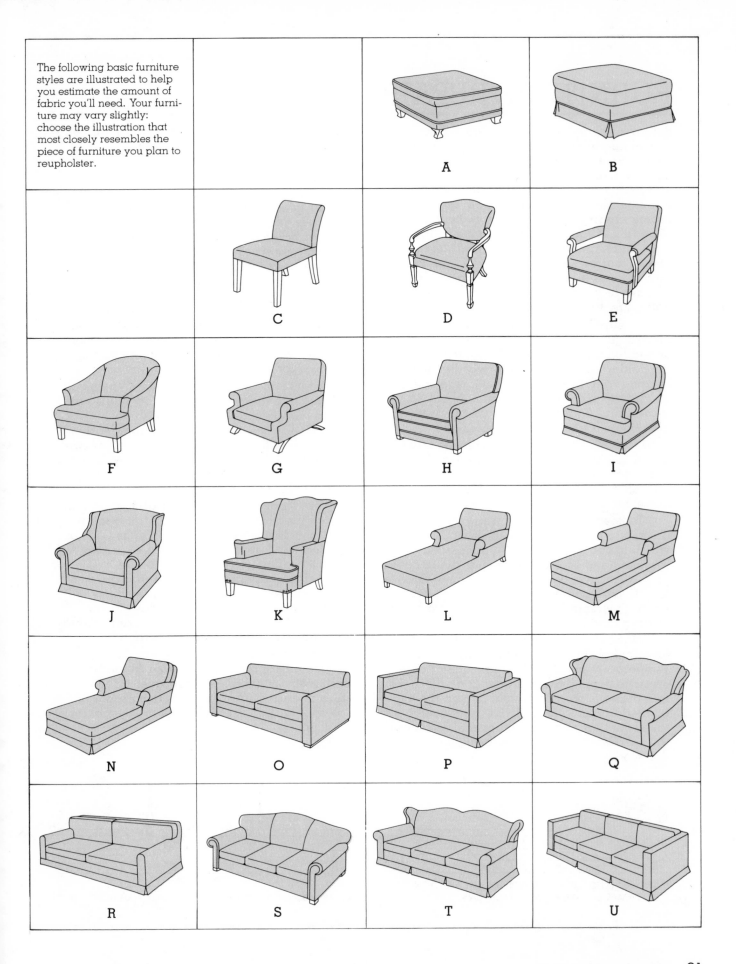

A

B

C

D

E

F

G

H

I

J

K

L

M

N

O

P

Q

R

S

T

U

FURNITURE REPAIR

Before reupholstering your piece of furniture, you should make sure its wooden frame is sound. Sometimes wobbles and squeaks will tell you at once that the frame needs fixing; in other situations, you may not discover frame troubles until you remove the old upholstery. Frame repair requires some woodworking expertise. If you find that you have neither the tools and expertise nor the inclination to tackle your own frame repair work, seek professional help in the Yellow Pages under "Furniture Repairing & Refinishing" before going any further with your project.

Tools & supplies. To knock apart the frame of a piece of furniture, you'll need a rubber mallet or padded hammer (for padding, try an old pot holder). If installing new wooden dowels becomes part of your task, you'll want to have an electric drill and an attachment called a "dowel bit." To repair an across-the-grain break, you'll also need a back saw.

When bonding two pieces of wood, use liquid aliphatic resin glue, known as "yellow glue," for a lasting bond. Add sawdust to thicken the glue, if you're working with dowels that are small for their holes.

To keep parts in place while the glue dries, you have four types of clamps from which to choose. Metal "C" clamps and wooden hand-screw clamps span distances of up to 18 inches; bar clamps expand to five feet. If you're gluing a part of a frame that is neither rectangular nor square, you may need to wrap it with a band clamp.

Wooden dowels hold glued breaks tighter for a longer time than metal screws. Temperature changes cause the metal of a screw to expand and contract at a different rate than the wooden frame, forcing the bonded fracture apart. If you use a dowel, take care that its diameter never exceeds half the narrowest dimension of the elements to be doweled.

Common frame repairs. Structural repairs on upholstered furniture involve either a loose joint, or a break in the frame. Four of the most common repair techniques follow.

Joints already strengthened by dowels are fairly easy to mend. After you've knocked the loose joint apart with a rubber mallet or padded hammer, try to twist the old dowels free with pliers. If this can't be done, you'll have to drill them out; make sure the diameter of your drill bit equals that of the dowels. Once you've scraped all surfaces free of old glue with an old knife blade or screwdriver tip, liberally apply aliphatic resin glue, and insert the new dowels (or reuse the old ones, scraped free of old glue). Clamp the parts together for 24 hours, to let the glue dry.

Some joints, such as those craftsmen call "tongue and groove," "through dovetail," and "open mortise and tenon," require no dowels—if you can knock them apart without breaking off their wooden ribs. If a rib or two break, you'll have to drill a small dowel hole through the joint and pin the joint with a dowel before regluing.

You'll need patience and skill to repair an across-the-grain frame break. After marking the frame for a 45° angled cut on either side of the shattered area, cut out the area with a back saw. Fashion an insert block of kiln-dried hardwood to replace the portion of the frame you removed. Clamp the block in place, then drill holes for four dowels, as shown below. Unclamp the block, apply glue to it, insert the dowels, and reclamp the whole assembly for 24 hours.

Count yourself lucky if your frame has split *with* the grain. In most cases, all you need to do is apply glue to both surfaces of the split wood, and clamp the break shut for 24 hours.

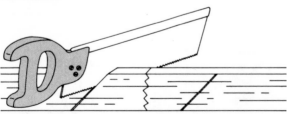

MARK 45° CUTS ON EITHER SIDE OF BREAK, THEN CUT OUT DAMAGED AREA WITH BACK SAW

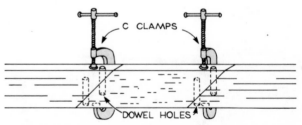

CLAMP WOODEN PIECES TOGETHER AND DRILL FOUR DOWEL HOLES

Measure, Shape & Sew

Though the fabric you select for the outer-cover sections of your furniture may be beautiful when you buy it, it will only be beautiful on your finished piece if it is carefully centered and fitted in place. Centering and fitting the outer cover are the two crucial determinants of your furniture's appearance. This chapter shows how to measure the fabric for your furniture's outer-cover sections, and how to center, match, and fit the sections to your piece. You'll also discover how to attach welt and boxing to outer-cover sections that need them.

Measuring your furniture

When planning your outer-cover sections, remember that everything—the exact yardage needed, the centering, the matching, shaping, and fitting of the sections—depends on how precisely you measure your furniture. It's important to measure the furniture before stripping it, when the original outer fabric is still in position, and to write all the measurements down. Our directions for measuring the furniture (and later for shaping and fitting the new fabric) assume that you are reupholstering your piece in its original style.

On pages 40–45, you'll find illustrated measurement lists for five types of commonly reupholstered furniture—ottomans, open-arm chairs, barrelback chairs, wing chairs, and fully upholstered armchairs. Each list shows where to write in your own measurements of your piece's decking (except in cases where there is no decking, as on ottomans and open-arm chairs) and of all the outer-cover sections.

As you fill in a list—ours or your own—make sure you measure and record each outer-cover section's greatest dimensions. For example, a T-shaped lip's greatest width occurs at the furniture's front, not between the inside arms, so you should plan to record the width of the lip at its widest point. You'll be cutting these maximum-dimension pieces from the fabric initially, then paring them down to shape as you fit them to the furniture's contours.

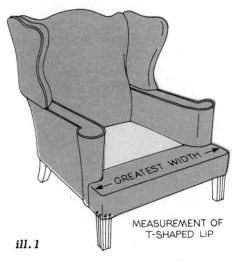

MEASUREMENT OF T-SHAPED LIP

GREATEST WIDTH

ill. 1

Two of the measurement lists contain the term "spring edge." Your furniture has a spring edge if its lip moves independently of the arm fronts when pushed down. Spring-edge lips require more fabric than non-spring-edge lips.

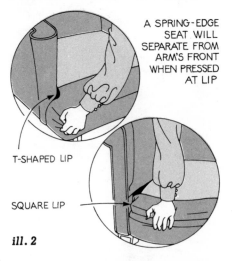

A SPRING-EDGE SEAT WILL SEPARATE FROM ARM'S FRONT WHEN PRESSED AT LIP

T-SHAPED LIP

SQUARE LIP

ill. 2

If your piece of furniture differs from any of those shown, compile your own list by selecting applicable features from different lists. For example, if you're reupholstering a tight-seat (cushionless) wing chair, combine the measurement advice from the barrelback chair, and wing chair lists.

No matter which style of furniture you plan to reupholster, take time to study the detailed measurement list for the fully upholstered armchair. This list—and only this list—explains all standard fabric allowances for seams, tacking, folding, etc. These allowances are especially crucial when you're planning to center and match a fabric with dominant motifs or stripes on any style of furniture (see page 35).

The list for the fully upholstered armchair can also be used as a guide in making your own list. Allow a column for the name of each outer-cover section (lip, inside back, outside arm, etc.); the number of sections of that description needed; and the length and width measurements of the section, including the standard allowances.

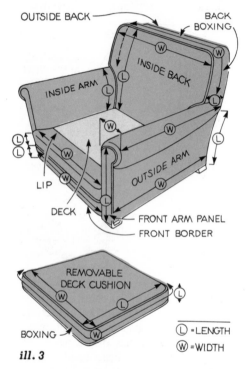

ill. 3

Measure the outer-cover sections in the order listed on pages 40–41. Hold one end of the tape measure firmly (or anchor it if the surface to be measured is greater than your extended arms' width) to one edge of the section to be measured. Then lay the tape across the fabric surface to the opposite edge of the section, pulling it as tight as you can without depressing the fabric surface. (Remember to measure each section at its widest and longest points.)

Unless you decide to leave your new cover weltless, measure all the seams and edges that boast welt. Divide the number of inches by 36 to obtain the linear yards of finished welt you'll need.

If you wish to determine how much fabric to buy, and haven't yet selected a fabric, use your measurements to draw a graph paper layout for nondominant-motif fabric—fabric that need not be centered or matched (directions follow). Be sure to add centering/matching percentages to the total fabric amount before you buy, if you end up selecting a fabric with dominant motifs or stripes.

If you've already selected a dominant-motif or striped fabric, buy a yard or two of it and use it as a sample to draw a graph paper layout for fabric that must be centered and matched (directions follow). This layout will show you *exactly* how much extra fabric you'll need and will assist you in centering and matching the dominant motifs or stripes when you begin to chalk and cut out your outer-cover sections (see pages 48–49).

Graph paper layouts

Rather than unroll the entire bolt of fabric on your floor or cutting table, plan a small-scale cutting layout on graph paper. Such a layout not only eases the task of chalking and cutting out fabric sections, but also reduces mistakes and helps achieve maximum economy in cutting. Always remember as you plan your layout that no two fabric sections should ever overlap on the layout.

Layouts for railroading fabric differ from those for running fabric vertically. When you plan a layout for railroading fabric, each outer-cover section's *length* determines how many sections you can fit into the fabric's width. When you plan a layout for running fabric vertically, each outer-cover section's *width* determines how many sections you can fit into the fabric's width. As

the Yardage Estimate Chart on pages 30–31 shows, railroading almost never consumes more fabric (except on high-back wing furniture)—and sometimes consumes less—than running fabric vertically. You can often use left-over yardage to rectify cutting mistakes. But remember that if your fabric has pile or vertically run designs, railroading is not possible.

Loose-leaf graph paper with four or five squares to the inch assists you in plotting exact measurements. Let each square represent two inches of fabric. For large chairs, you'll need to tape three or four sheets of graph paper together lengthwise; for sofas, you'll need to tape even more together. You'll also want a ruler, an eraser, a sharpened pencil, and your measurement list of section lengths and widths.

Whether you are drawing layouts for fabrics that needn't be centered or matched (sample layouts of this kind, one showing vertically run and the other railroaded fabric, are given on pages 46–47), or for fabrics boasting dominant motifs (a sample, showing vertically run fabric, is on the same pages), the following guidelines will help.

Step 1: Starting at bottom of graph paper, and ending at its top, draw parallel vertical lines to represent fabric's width, allowing each square to represent two inches of fabric. Close off bottom end with a horizontal line to represent bolt's free end; leave top end open.

Step 2: Along layout's right-hand margin, mark off each yard (every 18 squares) as you progress up the sheet.

Step 3: Nondominant motifs only: To maximize your chances of saving fabric, position most large outer-cover sections along the left-hand margin of your layout, tucking smaller sections into any space remaining at the right. The trick is to leave as little waste as possible along your fabric's width as you move slowly up your fabric's length from the layout's closed end. Lay similar sections side by side when you can. Be sure to pencil abbreviations of what the section is, and its measurements, in the center of each section on the layout. And remember *never* to allow two sections to overlap one another.

Step 4: Don't forget to allow fabric for welt. Draw diagonal lines (as shown on layouts on pages 46–47) through an area on the layout representing 1 square yard of fabric, to demark the fabric necessary for single welt on chairs and chaises. Allow approximately 1½ square yards for love seats, 1¾ square yards for sofas up to 84 inches wide, and 2¼ square yards for sofas up to 96 inches wide. You'll transform these diagonals into 1¾-inch-wide strips when you chalk your fabric. (Add 50 percent to these figures if you plan to use double welt.)

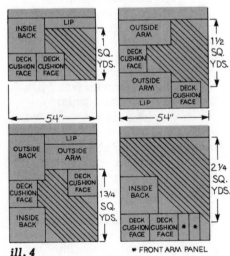

YOU CAN USE IRREGULARLY SHAPED AREAS FOR WELT STRIPS

ill. 4

* FRONT ARM PANEL

The area reserved for welt on the layout need not be square. In fact, you may be able to get several long strips by making use of irregularly shaped areas left free in your layout by the conformation of other sections.

When you finish your layout, scrutinize it for wasted areas. You may see ways to rearrange sections to conserve even more fabric.

Layouts for fabrics with dominant motifs or stripes. Your furniture will look best if you center dominant motifs on its front, seat, arms, and back, or match stripes along all its planes. If you plan to have a skirt, you'll also want to make sure that the skirt panel motifs match those on your furniture's front, sides, and back, using the principles on the following pages. Centering and matching require patience and plenty of fabric. If you run out of either, concentrate at least on centering motifs on the deck-cushion face(s) or tight seat, and on the inside arms and inside back.

ill. 5 SKIRT-PANEL MOTIFS SHOULD MATCH THOSE ON FRONT, SIDES, AND BACK

Centering the dominant motif on an outer-cover section means centering it on the part of the section which will be *visible* when the reupholstering is complete. For example, a chair's deck-cushion face is entirely visible but its inside back and arms are not—the cushion hides these sections' lower parts. When laying out the inside back and arms on your paper layout (and later chalking them on the fabric), you must deduct the deck cushion's thickness (its boxing's length) from the inside back and arm lengths to determine the lengths of their visible parts.

You must also deduct tacking or sewing allowances from the length and width of any outer-cover section whose allowances vary at its top, bottom, and sides (all standard fabric allowances are found in the measurement list for the fully upholstered armchair on pages 40–41). However, when a section such as a deck-cushion face has a uniform allowance on

DEDUCT CUSHION BOXING LENGTH TO CENTER MOTIF ON INSIDE ARM AND BACK

ill. 6

all sides, don't bother with deductions.

To center a motif along an outer-cover section's length, measure half the visible length of the section, adding the top tacking or sewing allowance above the motif's center, and draw a line to represent the section's top edge. Then measure the total length of the section down from this line and draw the section's bottom edge.

To center a motif across an outer-cover section's width, measure half the section's visible width, adding the side tacking or sewing allowance, on each side of the motif center. (Some inside-arm sections differ slightly—see page 38.)

Center dominant stripes as you would a dominant motif— along the section's width when the stripes are to run vertically, and along the section's length when the stripes are to be horizontal. Once the stripes are centered on each outer-cover section, the sections can be matched relatively easily.

CENTER DOMINANT STRIPE

ill. 7

To match dominant motifs, however, you must consider how the tacking or sewing allowances of two sections will come together. For example, the front boxing of a deck cushion should match the cushion face, but both have ½-inch seam allowances. You can't simply plot the boxing's length on your fabric layout, using the bottom edge of the cushion face as the top edge of the boxing, because when you cut out the two sections of fabric and sew them together, the combined seam allowances will crimp one inch out of the middle of your motif pattern, and the two pieces will not match properly.

Instead, you must position the cushion-face section over one motif center (drawn to scale on your layout—see page 46), making sure that the motif is properly centered on the cushion face. Then you must move to another motif center on your layout and position the cushion's front-boxing section over the new motif center. To do so, begin by sketching a line to represent the position of the cushion face's bottom edge in relation to the motif center. Then

MATCHING FRONT BOXING
TO CUSHION FACE ON LAYOUT

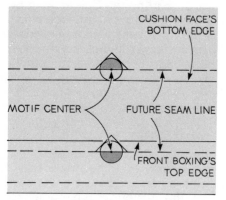

SHADED PORTIONS OF MOTIF
WILL SHOW WHEN PIECES ARE JOINED

ill. 8

measure one inch above that line (the combined seam allowances for both cushion face and boxing)

and draw the top edge of the front-boxing section. Erase the sketched line of the cushion face's bottom edge. Measure the boxing's total length down from its top edge and draw its bottom edge on your layout. Make sure that the boxing's motif is properly centered along the boxing's width, just as the cushion face's motif is centered along the face's width.

When you sew the two sections together, a ½ inch at the boxing's top edge and a ½ inch at the cushion face's bottom edge will be taken up in the seam and the two sections will match perfectly.

If you wish to have motifs flowing from the deck cushions to the back cushions on a sofa, you will have a similar matching problem; but in this case, you must consider the thickness (the boxing length) of the cushions as well as the seam allowances. You would plot the deck-cushion and back-cushion faces on your layout as you did the deck-cushion face and boxing above, but to the seam allowances, you would add the *back cushion's* thickness, if the back cushion rests on top of the deck cushion. If the pillow rests on the deck itself, behind the deck cushion, you would add the *deck cushion's* thickness to the seam allowances.

Lay out first those sections which require centering or matching. This means saving until last such items as cushion zipper boxings, hidden back boxings, and areas reserved for welt.

Though our step-by-step instructions deal with vertically run fabric, the same techniques apply to railroaded fabric (see sample layout for railroaded fabric on pages 46–47). To conserve fabric on your own piece of furniture, you may wish to arrange your sections in an order different from those shown on the sample layouts given for a fully upholstered armchair. The dotted lines on the sample layouts show where to sew stretchers on the inside back and the hidden back boxing at a later stage.

Step by step: Planning a vertically run, dominant-motif layout for a fully upholstered (skirtless) armchair

The steps that follow use standard fabric allowances (detailed in the fully upholstered armchair's measurement list on pages 40–41). The measurements and calculations in parentheses which accompany these steps were used to construct the sample layout on pages 46–47. They apply to a particular fully upholstered armchair and a 54-inch-wide bolt of fabric with very large dominant motifs, so don't forget to substitute your own measurements and fabric width (which may be narrower than 54 inches) as you move from step to step. Remember also that each square on your graph paper represents two inches of fabric.

Using the following steps, you will first measure the distances between dominant motifs and between the motifs and your bolt's free end and sides (excluding selvages). Next, you will sketch a representation of your fabric's motif pattern on your layout's graph paper. Last, you will position each fabric section on your layout so that the motifs appear in the section as you will want them on your furniture.

If you need to measure distances between one-direction motifs, be sure that the motifs point away from you (so that, once placed on your furniture, motifs will point up).

1 Write down and label three motif measurements made along your fabric's length. First, measure distance between your fabric's free (or cut) end and center of closest whole dominant motif (4¼ inches—see Line A in illustration 9). Second, if dominant motifs are staggered, measure distance between fabric's free (or cut) end and center of next closest dominant motif (16¼

inches—see Line B.) Finally, measure distance between one dominant motif's center and the next (25 inches—see Line C). This measurement defines the frequency with which the motif is repeated along fabric's length.

MEASURING FOR A VERTICALLY RUN, DOMINANT MOTIF LAYOUT

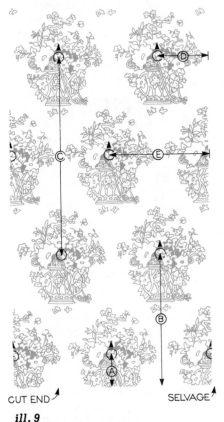

CUT END

SELVAGE

ill. 9

2 Write down and label two motif measurements made along your fabric's width (excluding selvages). First, measure distance from fabric's side to center of closest dominant motif (13½ inches—see Line D in illustration 9). Then, if dominant motifs are staggered, measure distance from fabric's side to center of next closest dominant motif (27 inches—see Line E).

3 Draw bolt of fabric on your graph paper layout, as explained in Steps 1 and 2 on page 34. Indicate all dominant-motif centers with circled dots, using

your motif-center measurements from the two steps above to calculate their positions.

You now have a scale drawing of your fabric, on which to position each outer-cover section so that your dominant motifs are centered and matched as they will appear on your furniture.

4 **Chair front.** If your fabric has such large dominant motifs that a single motif would nearly cover each visible plane of your furniture, plan to center the motif on your furniture's front. The term "front" includes both lip and front border or skirt. (Any fabric that has a less large dominant motif should have its motif centered only on the lip section of a piece of furniture, with the front-border section or skirt matched to the lip, using the technique discussed on pages 35–36.)

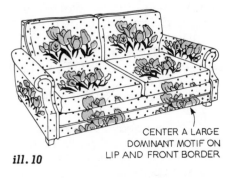

CENTER A LARGE DOMINANT MOTIF ON LIP AND FRONT BORDER

ill. 10

Below you will find an example, using the fully upholstered armchair, of how to plan your layout to center a very large motif on the front of your furniture—a process which is a little tricky. Take your time as you do it, and study the sample layout on pages 46–47 carefully.

Begin by obtaining visible lip length: the total length minus the horizontal part of lip that is hidden by deck cushion (14½ − 4 = 10½ inches), minus allowances (10½ − 2½ = 8 inches).

Next, obtain visible front-border length: the total front border length minus allowances (6 − 2½ = 3½ inches). Add visible lip length to visible front-border length (8 + 3½ = 11½ inches) to get total visible front length.

Now divide chair front's total

visible length by two (11½ ÷ 2 = 5¾ inches), to determine where to place center of motif on chair's front (5¾ inches up from this fully upholstered armchair front's bottom).

Next, you must calculate which part of the motif will appear on lip outer-cover section, in order to plot lip section on your layout. First, deduct front border's visible length (the total length minus allowances) from half of chair front's visible length (5¾ − 3½ = 2¼ inches). This tells you how far up on the lip from your furniture's visible lip bottom the motif center should be (2¼ inches).

Add lip's bottom tacking allowance to this number (2¼ + 2 = 4¼ inches) to find out how far below the center of a motif on your layout to draw bottom edge of lip's outer-cover section.

Measure lip's total length (14½ inches) up from lip's bottom edge; draw top edge of lip's section.

Since lip width allowances are the same on both sides, draw lip's sides on layout to left and right of motif center, each side half the total lip width (36 ÷ 2 = 18 inches) away from center.

Next, you must plot the position of front-border outer-cover section on your layout, so that the part of motif on front border will match that on lip. Add together lip's 2-inch bottom allowance and front border's ½-inch top allowance, to obtain total tacking allowance of 2½ inches. Moving to a different motif center on layout from the one over which lip section is positioned, sketch a line to represent position of lip's bottom edge below motif center (4¼ inches, as explained above). Measure 2½ inches above that line (the total tacking allowance length) and draw top edge of front-border section. Erase sketched line of lip's bottom edge.

Measure front border's total length (6 inches) down from its top edge; draw its bottom edge on layout.

Since front border's width allowances are the same on both sides, draw border's sides on layout to left and right of motif center, each side half the total border width (30 ÷ 2 = 15 inches) away from center.

5 Inside arms. Next on your layout, you should plan for inside-arm outer-cover sections (you need two). Determine visible inside-arm length: the total inside-arm length minus removable cushion's boxing length (37½ − 3½ = 34 inches), minus visible lip length obtained in previous step (34 − 8 = 26 inches), minus allowances (26 − 4 = 22 inches).

On some chairs, as on this fully upholstered armchair, the inside arm curves outward over arm's top, then under to meet the outside arm. The portion that curves under is hard to see, and should be deducted from the total visible length of inside arm. Measure length of curve from inside-arm top's outer edge to inside arm/outside arm junction (22 − 5 = 17 inches—see illustration 11).

MEASURING TO CENTER A MOTIF ON INSIDE ARM

① DEDUCT BACK BOXING DEPTH FOR HORIZONTAL CENTERING

⑤ CENTER MOTIF HORIZONTALLY

⑥ CENTER MOTIF VERTICALLY

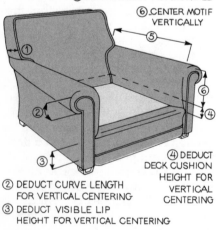

④ DEDUCT DECK CUSHION HEIGHT FOR VERTICAL CENTERING

② DEDUCT CURVE LENGTH FOR VERTICAL CENTERING
③ DEDUCT VISIBLE LIP HEIGHT FOR VERTICAL CENTERING

ill. 11

Divide the remaining visible length by two (17 ÷ 2 = 8½ inches). Add together half of inside arm's visible length, the top allowance, and the curve length (8½ + 2 + 5 = 15½ inches), measure this total distance above motif center, and draw top edge of inside-arm section. Measure inside arm's total length (37½ inches) down from top line and draw its bottom edge.

Visible inside-arm width is the total width minus allowances (39½ − 4 = 35½ inches). However, this fully upholstered armchair's T-shaped inside back covers part of inside arm's width, so the back boxing's visible length (6½ inches) must also be deducted from visible inside-arm width (35½ − 6½ = 29 inches).

Divide visible width by two (29 ÷ 2 = 14½ inches). Add allowance to this figure (14½ + 2 = 16½ inches), and use total to measure and draw left inside arm's front (left) edge on layout, to the left of motif center. Measure inside arm's total width (39½ inches) to the right of this line; draw left inside arm's rear (right) edge on layout.

Repeat above process for right inside arm, reversing measurements to the left and right of the motif center.

6 Inside back. Now move on to plot the inside-back outer-cover section on your layout. First, determine inside back's visible length: the total inside-back length minus deck cushion's boxing length (33½ − 3½ = 30 inches), minus allowances (30 − 2½ = 27½ inches).

Divide visible length by two (27½ ÷ 2 = 13¾ inches). Add together half of inside back's visible length, and the top allowance (13¾ + ½ = 14¼ inches); use total to measure and draw inside back's top edge above motif center. Measure inside back's total length down from this line, and draw its bottom edge.

Since inside back's width allowances are the same on both sides, draw its sides to the left and

right of motif center, each side half the total inside-back width (34 ÷ 2 = 17 inches) away from center.

7 Visible back boxing. To match the back boxing to the inside back, move to a different motif center on layout, and sketch a line to represent position of inside back's top edge above motif center (14¼ inches, as explained

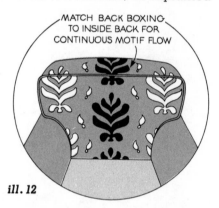

MATCH BACK BOXING TO INSIDE BACK FOR CONTINUOUS MOTIF FLOW

ill. 12

above). Measure one inch below that line (½ inch each for inside back's top and boxing's bottom seam allowance) and draw bottom edge of boxing section. Erase sketched line of inside back's top edge. Measure boxing's total length up from boxing's bottom edge, and draw its top edge. Since visible back boxing's width allowances are the same on both sides, draw its sides to the left and right of motif center, each side half the total back-boxing width (51 ÷ 2 = 25½ inches) away from center.

8 Outside arms. Next on your layout, plot the outside-arm outer-cover sections (you need two). If your fabric sports several different motifs, you can sometimes save yardage by centering a motif on the outside arms other than the dominant one used on the inside arms and back.

THE DOMINANT MOTIF ON OUTSIDE ARMS MAY BE DIFFERENT FROM OUTSIDE BACK OR INSIDE ARMS

ill. 13

Determine the visible outside-arm length: the total outside-arm length minus allowances (19 − 3 = 16 inches). Divide visible length by two (16 ÷ 2 = 8 inches). Add half of outside arm's visible length to its top allowance (8 + 1 = 9 inches); use this total to measure and draw outside arm's top edge above motif center. Measure arm's total length down from this line and draw its bottom edge.

Determine outside arm's visible width: the total width minus allowances (35 − 3 = 32 inches). Divide visible width by two (32 ÷ 2 = 16 inches). Add front allowance to this figure (16 + 1 = 17 inches), and use total to measure and draw right outside arm's front (left) edge on layout to the left of motif center. Measure right outside arm's total width (35 inches) to the right of this line, and draw right outside arm's rear (right) edge on layout.

Repeat above process for left outside arm, reversing measurements to the left and right of the motif center.

9 Outside back. If your fabric sports several different motifs, you can sometimes save yardage by centering on the outside back a motif other than the dominant one used on the inside arms and back. To position the outside-back outer-cover section on your layout, determine outside back's visible length: the total outside-back length minus allowances (34½ − 3 = 31½ inches). Divide visible length by two (31½ ÷ 2 = 15¾ inches). Add half of outside back's visible length to its top allowance (15¾ + 1 = 16¾ inches); use this total to measure and draw outside back's top edge above motif center. Measure outside back's total length down from this line and draw back's bottom edge.

CENTERING DOMINANT MOTIF ON OUTSIDE BACK

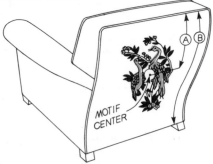

Ⓐ HALF VISIBLE LENGTH Ⓑ TOTAL VISIBLE LENGTH

ill. 14

Since outside back's width allowances are the same on both sides, draw its sides to the left and right of the motif center, each side half the outside back's total width (27½ ÷ 2 = 13¾ inches) away from center.

10 Deck cushion faces. Now plan the deck-cushion-face outer-cover sections on your layout (you need two). Since deck cushion face's length allowances are the same at top and bottom, draw its top and bottom edges above and below motif center, each edge half the deck cushion face's total length (25½ ÷ 2 = 12¾ inches) away from center.

Since deck cushion face's width allowances are the same on both sides, draw its sides to the right and left of the motif center, each side half the deck cushion face's total width (25½ ÷ 2 = 12¾ inches) away from center.

Repeat above process for second deck cushion face.

11 Deck cushion front boxing. To match the front boxing to the cushion face, move to a different motif center on layout, and sketch a line to represent position of cushion face's bottom edge below motif center (12¾ inches—as explained above). Measure

MATCH CUSHION FRONT BOXING TO MOTIF ON DECK CUSHION FACE FOR A CONTINUOUS DESIGN FLOW

ill. 15

three inches above that line (1½ inches each for cushion face's bottom and front boxing's top final shaping and seam allowance) and draw top edge of boxing section. Erase sketched line of cushion face's bottom edge. Measure boxing's total length down from boxing's top edge and draw its bottom edge.

Since deck cushion front boxing's width allowances are the same on both sides, draw its sides to the left and right of the motif center, each side half the front boxing's total width (53½ ÷ 2 = 26¾ inches) away from center.

12 Front arm panels. The same portion of the motif should appear in the same place on the left front arm panel as appears on the right one. However, you need not center a dominant motif on either arm panel; any portion of the fabric's pattern can be featured as long as the two panels look alike.

13 Welt. Fit welt area in wherever you can maximize number of long strips (see page 49).

14 Deck cushion zipper boxings. The zipper boxings (you need two) on a deck cushion

(Continued on page 48)

MEASUREMENT LISTS

Use one of these lists — or make up your own from components of several — to record the greatest length and width of each outer-cover section on your furniture. Then plot the sections on a paper layout as described on pages 34–39. The layout will show how much fabric you need, and help you avoid cutting mistakes.

Though you'll find the standard fabric allowances for seams, tacking, folding, etc. included in each of the five ready-made lists that follow, only one list — that for the fully upholstered armchair — explains all the allowances in detail. It is crucial to understand these allowances if you're planning to center and match a fabric with dominant motifs or stripes. No matter what style of furniture you're reupholstering, use the fully upholstered armchair's explanations as your allowance guide.

Note: If your furniture is to have a skirt, be sure to measure the skirt width at the skirt's top-edge height on your furniture.

FULLY UPHOLSTERED ARMCHAIR
with spring-edge lip and rectangular cushion

Deck	**Decking (denim or muslin)**	
	Measure from 4 to 5. Add 2½ inches (½ inch for seam at front, 2 inches for tacking at back).	L: _____
	Measure from 3 to 4. Add 4 inches (2 inches for tacking on each side).	W: _____
Skirt front	**Outer cover**	
	Measure from 1 to 2. Add 1 inch (½ inch for seam at bottom, ½ inch for blind-tacking or blind-stitching at top).	L: _____
	Measure from 3 to 4. Add 9 inches (½ inch for seam and 4 inches for folding on each side).	W: _____
Skirt back	Measure from 1 to 2. Add 1 inch (½ inch for seam at bottom, ½ inch for blind-tacking or blind-stitching at top).	L: _____
	Measure from 5 to outside edge of fourth leg at back (not shown). Add 9 inches (½ inch for seam and 4 inches for folding on each side).	W: _____
Skirt sides (need two)	Measure from 1 to 2. Add 1 inch (½ inch for seam at bottom, ½ inch for blind-tacking or blind-stitching at top).	L: _____
	Measure from 4 to 5. Add 9 inches (½ inch for seam and 4 inches for folding on each side).	W: _____
Skirt pleat backdrops (need four)	Measure from 1 to 2. Add 1 inch (½ inch for seam at bottom, ½ inch for tacking at top).	L: _____
	Pleat backdrops are 9 inches wide.	W: _9"_
Front border (skip if skirt is used)	Measure from 6 to 7. Add 2½ inches (½ inch for blind-tacking at top, 2 inches for tacking under at bottom).	L: _____
	Measure from 8 to 9. Add 4 inches (2 inches for tacking on each side).	W: _____
Lip (if skirt is not used)	Measure from 6 to 10. Add 2½ inches (½ inch for seam at top, 2 inches for tacking at bottom).	L: _____
	Measure from 8 to 9. Add twice the distance between 10 and 11 (to allow fabric to go around corners of spring-edge lip).	W: _____
Lip (if skirt is used)	Measure from 7 to 10. Add 2½ inches (½ inch for seam at top, 2 inches for tacking under at bottom).	L: _____
	Measure from 8 to 9. Add twice the distance between 10 and 11 (to allow fabric to go around corners of spring-edge lip).	W: _____
Inside arm (need two)	Measure from 12 to 13. Add 4 inches (2 inches for tacking at top, 2 inches for tacking at bottom).	L: _____
	Measure from 14 to 15. Add 4 inches (2 inches for tacking at front edge, 2 inches for tacking at back edge).	W: _____

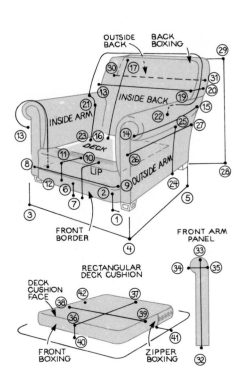

Inside back	Measure from 16 to 17. Add 2½ inches (½ inch for seam at top, 2 inches for attaching stretcher to bottom).	L: _____
	Measure from 18 to 19. Add 4 inches (2 inches for final shaping on each side).	W: _____
Visible back boxing	Measure from 19 to 20 (front-to-back length of back boxing where it meets top of inside arm). Add 2½ inches (½ inch for seam at inside-back edge, 2 inches for tacking at outside-back edge).	L: _____
	Measure from 21 to 22. Add 1 inch (½ inch for seam on each side).	W: _____
Hidden back boxing (need two)	Measure from 19 to 20. Add 2½ inches (½ inch for seam at inside-back edge, 2 inches for attaching stretcher to outside-back edge).	L: _____
	Measure from 21 to 23. Add ½ inch (for seam at top).	W: _____
Outside arm (need two)	Measure from 24 to 25. Add 3 inches (1 inch for blind-tacking at top, 2 inches for tacking under at bottom).	L: _____
	Measure from 26 to 27 (across outside arm's top). Add 3 inches (1 inch for tacking at front edge, 2 inches for tacking at back edge).	W: _____
Outside back	Measure from 28 to 29. Add 3 inches (1 inch for blind-tacking at top, 2 inches for tacking under at bottom).	L: _____
	Measure from 30 to 31. Add 2 inches (1 inch for blind-stitching on each side).	W: _____
Front arm panel (need two)	Measure from 32 to 33. Add 2 inches (1 inch for tacking at top, 1 inch for tacking at bottom).	L: _____
	Measure from 34 to 35. Add 2 inches (1 inch for tacking on each side).	W: _____
Deck cushion face (need two)	Measure from 36 to 37. Add 3 inches (1½ inches each at front and back edges for final shaping and seam).	L: _____
	Measure from 38 to 39. Add 3 inches (1½ inches on each side for final shaping and seam).	W: _____
Deck cushion front boxing	Measure from 36 to 40. For fabrics that don't need to be centered or matched, add 1 inch (½ inch for top and bottom seams). For fabrics that need to be centered or matched, add 2 inches (1½ inches for top edge's final shaping and seam, ½ inch for bottom edge's seam).	L: _____
	Measure from 41 to 42, around cushion front. Add 4 inches (½ inch for seam and 1½ inches for overlap on each side).	W: _____
Deck cushion zipper boxing (need two)	Measure from 36 to 40. Divide measurement by 2; add 1½ inches (½ inch for seam, 1 inch for zipper fold).	L: _____
	Measure from 41 to 42, around cushion back. Add 1 inch (½ inch for seam on each side).	W: _____

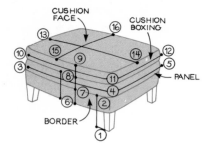

OTTOMAN with attached cushion

	Outer cover	
Skirt sides (need two)	Measure from 1 to 2. Add 1 inch.	L: _____
	Measure from 3 to 4. Add 9 inches.	W: _____
Skirt ends (need two)	Measure from 1 to 2. Add 1 inch.	L: _____
	Measure from 4 to 5. Add 9 inches.	W: _____
Skirt pleat backdrops (need four)	Measure from 1 to 2. Add 1 inch.	L: _____
	Pleat backdrops are 9 inches wide.	W: __9"__
Border sides (need two— skip if skirt is used)	Measure from 6 to 7. Add 2½ inches (½ inch for blind-tacking at top, 2 inches for tacking under at bottom).	L: _____
	Measure from 3 to 4. Add 1 inch (½ inch for seam on each side).	W: _____
Border ends (need two— skip if skirt is used)	Measure from 6 to 7. Add 2½ inches (same as border sides).	L: _____
	Measure from 4 to 5. Add 1 inch (same as border sides).	W: _____
Panel sides (if skirt is used— need two)	Measure from 6 to 8. Add 5½ inches (3½ inches for seam and hidden part of panel at top, 2 inches for tacking under at bottom).	L: _____
	Measure from 3 to 4. Add 1 inch (½ inch for seam on each side).	W: _____
Panel ends (if skirt is used— need two)	Measure from 6 to 8. Add 5½ inches (same as panel sides).	L: _____
	Measure from 4 to 5. Add 1 inch (same as panel sides).	W: _____
Panel sides (if skirt is not used— need two)	Measure from 7 to 8. Add 5½ inches (3½ inches for seam and hidden part of panel at top, 2 inches for tacking under at bottom).	L: _____
	Measure from 3 to 4. Add 1 inch.	W: _____
Panel ends (if skirt is not used— need two)	Measure from 7 to 8. Add 5½ inches (same as panel sides).	L: _____
	Measure from 4 to 5. Add 1 inch (same as panel sides).	W: _____
Cushion boxing sides (need two)	Measure from 8 to 9. Add 1 inch.	L: _____
	Measure from 10 to 11. Add 1 inch (½ inch for seam on each side).	W: _____
Cushion boxing ends (need two)	Measure from 8 to 9. Add 1 inch.	L: _____
	Measure from 11 to 12. Add 1 inch (same as boxing sides).	W: _____
Cushion face (need two)	Measure from 13 to 14. Add 2 inches (1 inch each at front and back edges for final shaping and seam).	L: _____
	Measure from 15 to 16. Add 2 inches (1 inch on each side for final shaping and seam).	W: _____

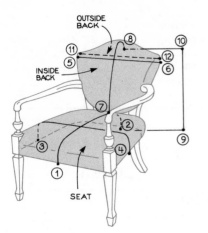

OPEN-ARM CHAIR with crowned seat

	Outer cover		
Seat	Measure from 1 to 2. Add 4 inches.	L: _____	
	Measure from 3 to 4. Add 4 inches.	W: _____	
Inside back	Measure from 7 to 8 (where inside back meets outside back). Add 4 inches.	L: _____	
	Measure from 5 to 6. Add 4 inches.	W: _____	
Outside back	Measure from 9 to 10. Add 3 inches.	L: _____	
	Measure from 11 to 12. Add 2 inches.	W: _____	

FULLY UPHOLSTERED BARRELBACK CHAIR
with T-shaped tight seat

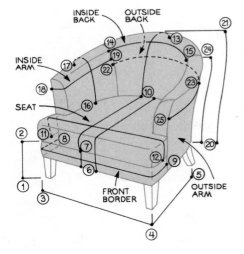

	Outer cover		
Skirt front	Measure from 1 to 2. Add 1 inch.	L: _____	
	Measure from 3 to 4. Add 9 inches.	W: _____	
Skirt sides (need two)	Measure from 1 to 2. Add 1 inch.	L: _____	
	Measure from 4 to 5. Add 9 inches.	W: _____	
Skirt back	Measure from 1 to 2. Add 1 inch.	L: _____	
	Measure from 5 to outside edge of fourth leg at back (not shown). Add 9 inches.	W: _____	
Skirt pleat back-drops (need four)	Measure from 1 to 2. Add 1 inch.	L: _____	
	Pleat backdrops are 9 inches wide.	W: *9"*	
Front border (skip if skirt is used)	Measure from 6 to 7. Add 2½ inches.	L: _____	
	Measure from 8 to 9. Add 4 inches.	W: _____	
Seat (if border is used, but not skirt)	Measure from 7 to 10. Add 4 inches (2 inches for tacking under at front edge, 2 inches for attaching stretcher to back edge).	L: _____	
	Measure from 11 to 12. Add 4 inches.	W: _____	
Seat (if no border is used; skirt optional)	Measure from 6 to 10. Add 4 inches (2 inches for tacking under at front edge, 2 inches for attaching stretcher to back edge).	L: _____	
	Measure from 11 to 12. Add 4 inches.	W: _____	
Inside back	Measure from 10 to 13 (where inside back meets outside back). Add 4 inches (2 inches for tacking at top, 2 inches for attaching stretcher to bottom).	L: _____	
	Measure from 14 to 15. Add 4 inches (2 inches for attaching stretcher to each side).	W: _____	
Inside arm (need two)	Measure from 16 to 17 (where inside arm meets outside arm). Add 4 inches (same as inside back).	L: _____	
	Measure from 18 to 19. Add 4 inches (2 inches for tacking at front edge, 2 inches for attaching stretcher to back edge).	W: _____	

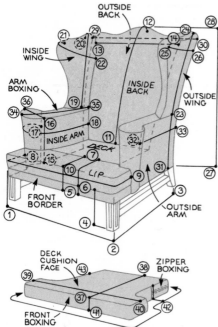

Outside back	Measure from 20 to 21. Add 3 inches.	L: _____
	Measure from 22 to 23. Add 2 inches.	W: _____
Outside arm (need two)	Measure from 24 to 20. Add 3 inches.	L: _____
	Measure from 25 to 23. Add 3 inches.	W: _____

FULLY UPHOLSTERED WING CHAIR
with spring-edge lip and T-shaped cushion

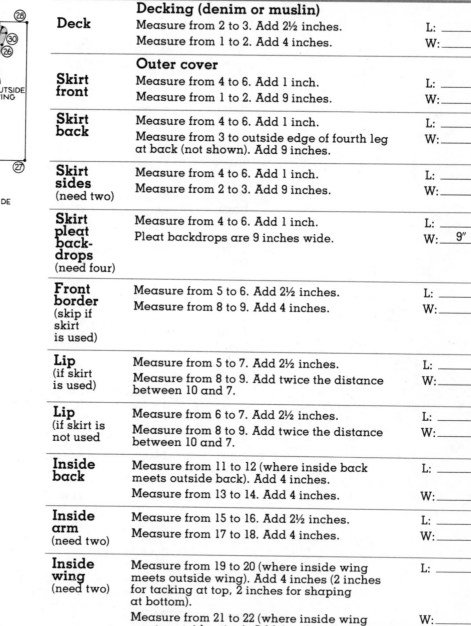

Deck	**Decking (denim or muslin)**	
	Measure from 2 to 3. Add 2½ inches.	L: _____
	Measure from 1 to 2. Add 4 inches.	W: _____
Skirt front	**Outer cover**	
	Measure from 4 to 6. Add 1 inch.	L: _____
	Measure from 1 to 2. Add 9 inches.	W: _____
Skirt back	Measure from 4 to 6. Add 1 inch.	L: _____
	Measure from 3 to outside edge of fourth leg at back (not shown). Add 9 inches.	W: _____
Skirt sides (need two)	Measure from 4 to 6. Add 1 inch.	L: _____
	Measure from 2 to 3. Add 9 inches.	W: _____
Skirt pleat backdrops (need four)	Measure from 4 to 6. Add 1 inch.	L: _____
	Pleat backdrops are 9 inches wide.	W: _9"_
Front border (skip if skirt is used)	Measure from 5 to 6. Add 2½ inches.	L: _____
	Measure from 8 to 9. Add 4 inches.	W: _____
Lip (if skirt is used)	Measure from 5 to 7. Add 2½ inches.	L: _____
	Measure from 8 to 9. Add twice the distance between 10 and 7.	W: _____
Lip (if skirt is not used)	Measure from 6 to 7. Add 2½ inches.	L: _____
	Measure from 8 to 9. Add twice the distance between 10 and 7.	W: _____
Inside back	Measure from 11 to 12 (where inside back meets outside back). Add 4 inches.	L: _____
	Measure from 13 to 14. Add 4 inches.	W: _____
Inside arm (need two)	Measure from 15 to 16. Add 2½ inches.	L: _____
	Measure from 17 to 18. Add 4 inches.	W: _____
Inside wing (need two)	Measure from 19 to 20 (where inside wing meets outside wing). Add 4 inches (2 inches for tacking at top, 2 inches for shaping at bottom).	L: _____
	Measure from 21 to 22 (where inside wing meets outside wing). Add 4 inches (2 inches for tacking on each side).	W: _____

Outside wing (need two)	Measure from 23 to 24. Add 3 inches (1 inch for blind-stitching at top, 2 inches for tacking at bottom).	L: _____
	Measure from 25 to 26. Add 3 inches (1 inch for blind-stitching at front edge, 2 inches for tacking at back edge).	W: _____
Outside back	Measure from 27 to 28. Add 3 inches.	L: _____
	Measure from 29 to 30. Add 2 inches.	W: _____
Outside arm (need two)	Measure from 31 to 23. Add 3 inches.	L: _____
	Measure from 32 to 33. Add 3 inches.	W: _____
Arm boxing (need two)	Measure from 34 to 35. Add 4 inches.	L: _____
	Measure from 36 to 16. Add 4 inches.	W: _____
Deck cushion face (need two)	Measure from 37 to 38. Add 3 inches.	L: _____
	Measure from 39 to 40. Add 3 inches.	W: _____
Deck cushion front boxing	Measure from 37 to 41. Add 1 inch for fabrics that don't need to be centered or matched, 2 inches for fabrics that do.	L: _____
	Measure from 42 to 43, around cushion front. Add 4 inches.	W: _____
Deck cushion zipper boxing (need two)	Measure from 37 to 41. Divide measurement by 2; add 1½ inches.	L: _____
	Measure from 42 to 43, around cushion back. Add 1 inch.	W: _____

These are sample layouts, representing the outer covers of fully upholstered armchairs, mapped out three different ways on two types of fabric. Each was prepared following the guidelines on pages 34–35, in order to demonstrate the most economical use of fabric, and—on the layout for dominant-motif fabric—to show in detail a solution to the centering and matching problems of one furnishing's outer cover. Use these as guides as you plan your own graph paper layout.

The bolts of fabric portrayed in the samples are all 54 inches wide; yours may be narrower.

You'll notice that the two layouts on the left have skirts, while the dominant-motif layout on the right has a front border, in order to show you as many variations as possible.

Two of these layouts portray vertically run fabric; one portrays railroaded fabric. Remember that if you railroad your fabric, the outer-cover sections' *widths* should parallel the fabric's selvages on your layout; their *lengths* should parallel the selvages if your fabric is to be vertically run.

On all layouts the word "welt" means single welt. For double welt, increase the space allotted for welt by 50 percent. The layouts' shaded areas show fabric waste; the dotted lines on the inside backs and hidden back boxings show where to attach stretchers.

The dominant-motif layout has additional symbols. Each ⊙ shows a dominant-motif center. Short, solid lines mark off tacking and sewing allowances. Short lines, broken in half, on the front border, visible back boxing, and deck-cushion front boxing, indicate lines that were sketched in to help in the matching process, then erased once the matching was completed.

Here is a list of the abbreviations used on all three layouts:

HBB: Hidden back boxing
VBB: Visible back boxing
DCF: Deck-cushion face
DCFB: Deck-cushion front boxing
DCZB: Deck-cushion zipper boxing
FAP: Front arm panel
FB: Front border
IA: Inside arm
IB: Inside back
L: Length
OA: Outside arm
OB: Outside back
SB: Skirt back
SF: Skirt front
SPB: Skirt pleat backdrop
SS: Skirt side
W: Width

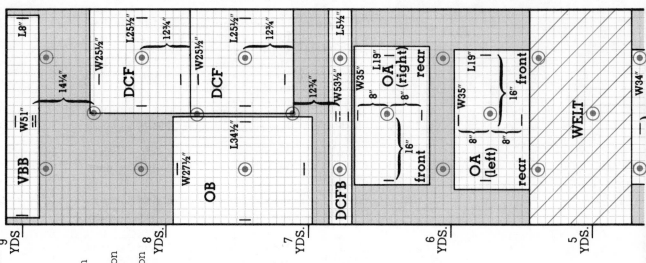

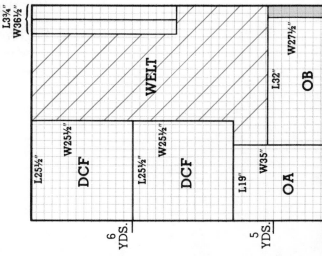

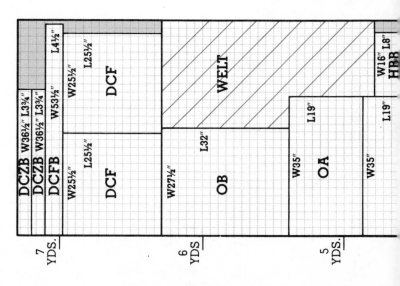

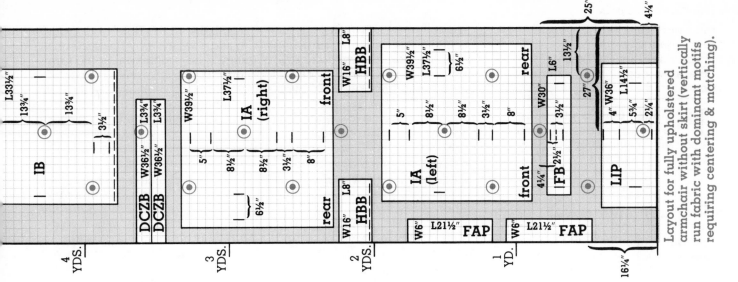

Layout for fully upholstered armchair without skirt (vertically run fabric with dominant motifs requiring centering & matching).

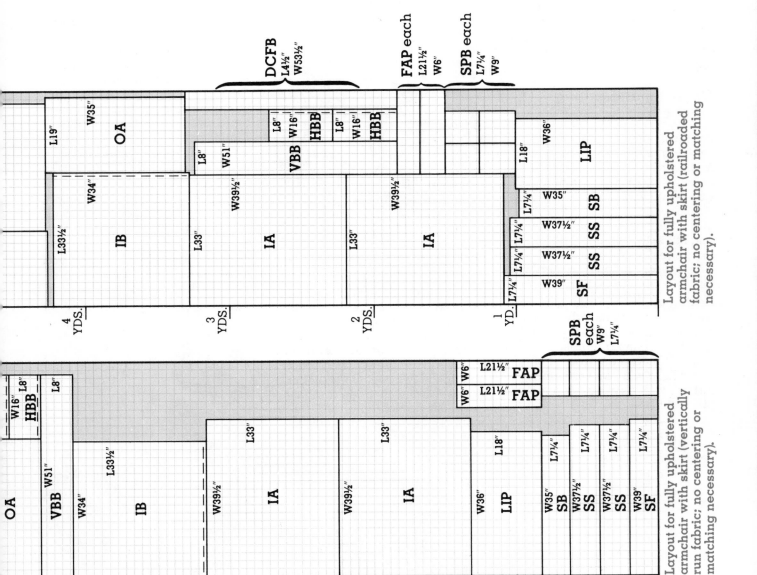

Layout for fully upholstered armchair with skirt (railroaded fabric; no centering or matching necessary).

Layout for fully upholstered armchair with skirt (vertically run fabric; no centering or matching necessary).

Paper Layouts   47

. . . Continued from page 39

are hidden from view at cushion's rear, so motif placement on them is not important. Fit boxing outer-cover sections in wherever you have room on your layout.

15 Hidden back boxings. Fit hidden back boxings (you need two) in wherever you have room on your layout.

Shaping outer cover

Precisely cut outer-cover sections are essential if you are to achieve the professional look you want on your reupholstered furniture. The following pages tell you how to chalk and cut outer-cover sections, welt, and stretchers, and how to shape and fit certain types of sections to your furniture before sewing them.

Chalking and cutting outer cover

For most outer-cover sections, chalking and cutting simply means transferring your paper layout—expanded to actual size—onto your outer-cover fabric. Some sections, however, require additional special shaping and fitting techniques. The following pages explain these techniques, and offer general tips for chalking and cutting.

Setting up. Your chalking and shaping operations may last several hours, especially if your fabric boasts dominant motifs or stripes. Choose an area for cutting where you can work undisturbed, with easy access to your piece of furniture.

You'll need a firm surface on which to chalk and cut your fabric. Use a clean hardwood floor, or place a smooth 4 by 8-foot sheet of ½ to 1-inch-thick plywood over your carpet. Better yet, set the plywood sheet on a large table, to save your back from strain as you work.

You'll also need a yardstick, shears, upholstery skewers, your paper layout, your measurement list (necessary if your fabric has dominant motifs), and blackboard chalk—white for dark fabrics and yellow for light-colored fabrics.

How to chalk and cut. Chalk, cut, and fit one outer-cover section at a time; it's easier to handle a whole bolt of fabric this way. You can also match the dominant

CUTTING FABRIC SECTIONS SO MOTIFS MATCH

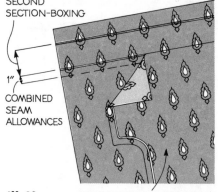

SECOND
SECTION–BOXING

1"

COMBINED
SEAM
ALLOWANCES

ill. 16   FIRST SECTION – INSIDE BACK

motifs on two adjoining sections relatively easily by cutting the first section out and moving it over the uncut fabric until the first section's motif lines up over another motif, then chalking the second section so that the two sections' adjoining edges will match when their allowances are folded under. Remember as you match motifs to leave space for the allowances, just as you did when centering and matching your fabric's motifs or stripes on your paper layout (see page 35).

In general, you should chalk each section's outline on the right side of your fabric. Cut it out and, on the fabric's wrong side, label it with the section's name and mark

it with the words "top" and "front" to show which way the section should be positioned on the furniture. If the section needs no special shaping or fitting, set it aside and begin to chalk the next section. If a section needs more shaping or fitting (see pages 49–52), you'll be doing more chalking right on your furniture.

When chalking, watch out for pile fabrics. Velvets, velours, and corduroys have pile that naturally lies in one direction. When you run your hand in this direction, the pile smooths down; when you run your hand in the opposite direction, it stands up.

You must be careful to plan, chalk, and cut the outer-cover sections so that the pile on all sections smooths either toward the floor or toward the front of your furniture when the sections are fitted into place on the furniture. Should you err and cut a section in a contrasting direction, it's better to discard it and cut another than to risk having sections whose piles lie in opposing directions show up as slightly different colors on your finished piece.

The following tips will ease your chalking and cutting chores.

Step 1: Before you begin chalking, check fabric for straight lines of weave. If selvages pucker or motifs do not follow a straight line, work selvages down toward

WAYS TO STRAIGHTEN UNEVEN FABRIC WEAVE

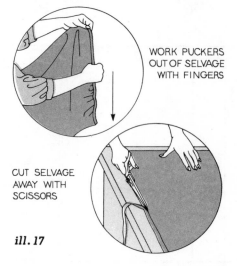

WORK PUCKERS
OUT OF SELVAGE
WITH FINGERS

CUT SELVAGE
AWAY WITH
SCISSORS

ill. 17

bolt's free end, or cut selvages off to release fabric (see illustration 17).

Step 2: Chalk a line along a weft yarn (a yarn that runs across fabric's width) before measuring and chalking an outer-cover section. Then measure and chalk section from this base line. The line itself may not be ruler-straight, but the section's edge will be straight once you cut along it.

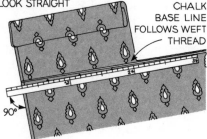

SECTION'S BASE LINE MAY NOT LOOK STRAIGHT

CHALK BASE LINE FOLLOWS WEFT THREAD

90°

YARDSTICK, WHEN PLACED AT A 90° ANGLE TO SELVAGE, MAY NOT FOLLOW WEFT THREAD

ill. 18

Step 3: Double-check all your measurements against layout and measurement list. Then measure and mark each section's length and width at several points to insure precise chalking.

Step 4: Keep chalk point sharp; you can use shears to pare it. Chalk thin, light lines—they insure accurate cutting and brush off easily if you make a mistake.

Step 5: Draw along your yardstick as you measure and chalk outlines. Try to measure sections precisely—to the ¼ inch.

Step 6: Cut right down the middle of each chalk line. Shape or fit each section as it is cut (if necessary—see pages 49–52), label it, and set it aside until you've cut and fit all sections. Page 52 tells you how to keep cut sections in order.

Step 7: When working with loosely woven fabrics, put ¼-inch-wide masking tape along cut edges to prevent unravelling.

Cutting welt. We recommend making both single and double welt from diagonally cut strips. Called "bias welt," it hugs curves and prevents the pile from separating on velvets or velours.

To cut bias strips for welt from a rectangular fabric section, measure the length of one side edge of the section available for welt (Point A to Point B in illustration 19), then measure and mark the same dimension (Point A to Point C in illustration 19) across the section's width at its bottom edge. Draw a diagonal line joining the section's top corner with

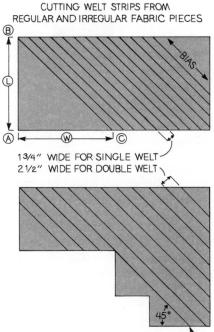

CUTTING WELT STRIPS FROM REGULAR AND IRREGULAR FABRIC PIECES

B

L

BIAS

A   W   C

1¾" WIDE FOR SINGLE WELT
2½" WIDE FOR DOUBLE WELT

45°

LONGEST POSSIBLE DIAGONAL LINE

ill. 19

the mark at the bottom edge (Point B to Point C). This diagonal line forms the base for all your bias cuts.

To cut bias strips from a fabric section neither square nor rectangular, draw the longest possible diagonal line through the section at an approximate 45° angle to the weave, to form the base line.

Whether your welt section is rectangular or irregular, chalk

lines parallel to the base line 1¾ inch apart for single welt and 2½ inches apart for double welt. Cut along these lines. As you cut each welt strip, line it up along your yardstick until you have measured off the total linear yardage needed for your finished welt. Then cut an extra two yards of strips to cover piecing and handling.

Note: Piecing bias strips together to make a continuous length works fine for single welt. But in making double welt, especially of heavier fabrics, piecing may create noticeable lumps in the finished piece. To avoid this problem, try to cut single long bias strips to fit each section of your furniture.

Cutting stretchers. Cut stretchers from any old or new scraps of sturdy fabric. Measure each section edge to which a stretcher will be sewn; this length will determine the length of that edge's stretcher. Though stretcher lengths vary according to the length of the edges to which they will be attached, all stretcher widths should be approximately eight inches wide.

Information on how to attach stretchers to particular sections can be found under "Machine-sewing parts of outer cover," page 52. You often need stretchers for the bottom and side edges of the inside-back outer-cover sections of the fully upholstered pieces shown in the measurement lists. You also need them for the bottom and back edges of the wing-chair inside-arm sections.

Fitting techniques

The following information is for outer-cover sections that must be fitted individually before the cover is put on the furniture. (Though you need special techniques for cutting and fitting loose cushions and skirts as well, you shape these sections during and after reupholstering your piece.)

Remember to mark ½-inch seam allowances on all edges of fitted sections to which other pieces will be sewn.

If your fabric stretches easily, stretch each section slightly and pin or tape it to your cutting surface before doing the final cutting.

T-shaped inside back. Place the outer-cover section over the inside back of your chair or sofa; center it so that it has the correct allowances on all sides. Pin it in place with four upholsterer's skewers or standard dressmaker's pins, placed as close to the top and bottom edges as possible. Starting at a top corner, trace the side edges of the inside back with sharpened chalk. Make diagonal cuts into the fabric along the arm top's inner curve, where the inside back narrows, cutting *just* until the fabric lies flat against the back. You may need to make two or more cuts on each side. Do *not* cut into the chalk outline of the inside-back edges.

Take the section off the chair, place it on the cutting surface and refine the chalk outline of the inside back's edges. Trim off any excess fabric, leaving a 1-inch-wide allowance around all edges.

Place the section on the chair again to check for accurate shaping. If necessary, refine the chalk line again. Then clip the top corners of the inside-back section to prevent them from looking too

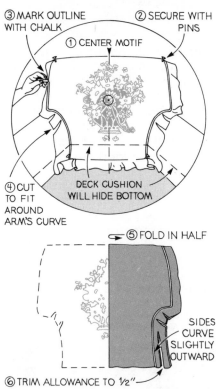

SHAPING T-SHAPED INSIDE BACK

③ MARK OUTLINE WITH CHALK
② SECURE WITH PINS
① CENTER MOTIF
④ CUT TO FIT AROUND ARM'S CURVE
DECK CUSHION WILL HIDE BOTTOM

⑤ FOLD IN HALF
SIDES CURVE SLIGHTLY OUTWARD
⑥ TRIM ALLOWANCE TO ½"

ill. 20

pointed when the outer cover is sewn and put on the furniture. To clip the corners, measure and mark 2½ inches in toward the center of the top edge from each corner, and down ¼ inch from each corner along the side edges. Join the ¼-inch mark to the 2½-inch mark at each corner with a slightly convex curved line. Cut along the line at each corner.

Fold the section in half along its length and cut around the chalk lines, shaping both sides together (leave a ½-inch allowance around the outside of the chalk line). This insures a uniform curve on both sides. The sides of the inside back, near the bottom edge, should curve slightly outward.

Turn the section wrong side up. Chalk a ½-inch seam line on all four sides. Later, you'll sew back boxing to the inside back's top and sides, and stretchers to its side boxings and bottom edge.

Spring-edge lips. Spring-edge lips may be rectangular (such as the one on the fully upholstered armchair used throughout this

book) or T-shaped (such as the one on the wing chair, page 33).

To fit an outer-cover section to a rectangular spring-edge lip, fold the lip in half along its length and notch the fold at the top to mark the lip's center. To either side of the notch, measure and mark half of the lip's width (minus allowances).

Cut the lip corners out at an angle to hide the later corner seams below deck level. To do so, begin at the mark to the notch's right, and measure 4¾ inches down from the lip's top edge; mark with chalk. Chalk another mark ¾ inch to the right of the first mark, along the top edge. Chalk a straight line joining the last mark and the one 4¾ inches down from top edge.

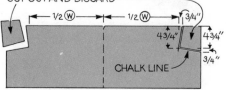

CUT OUT AND DISCARD
½ W
½ W
¾"
4¾"
4¾"
¾"
CHALK LINE

FITTING RECTANGULAR SPRING-EDGE LIP
ill. 21

Now measure 4¾ inches down along the lip's right edge; mark. Chalk another mark ¾ inch below this one and join it to the bottom of the first line with another straight line. Cut along both chalk lines.

Repeat the procedure to cut out the lip's left corner, substituting the word "left" for the word "right."

To fit an outer-cover section to a T-shaped spring-edge lip, place the fabric section on the lip of chair or sofa, centering it so that it has correct allowances on all sides. Be sure the side allowances extend past the line where the inside arm meets the outside arm, around the arm fronts. Pin the section to the chair's deck and front with four upholsterer's skewers or standard dressmaker's pins; pin it to the chair's sides with two skewers or pins on each side.

Smooth the fabric out toward the lip edge and pin a dart along the edge as shown in illustration 22. Trim the dart to within a ½ inch of the pins.

At the point where the inside arm begins to curve out, snip the fabric to within one inch of the deck (see illustration 22). This allows the fabric to lie flat around the lip/deck curve. Chalk the lip/deck curve around the arm front. Repeat the procedure on the lip's other side.

FITTING T-SHAPED SPRING-EDGE LIP

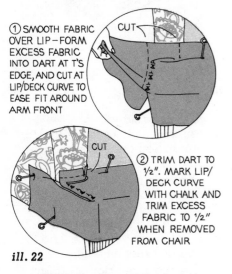

① SMOOTH FABRIC OVER LIP—FORM EXCESS FABRIC INTO DART AT T'S EDGE, AND CUT AT LIP/DECK CURVE TO EASE FIT AROUND ARM FRONT

② TRIM DART TO ½". MARK LIP/DECK CURVE WITH CHALK AND TRIM EXCESS FABRIC TO ½" WHEN REMOVED FROM CHAIR

ill. 22

On both sides of the lip, trim the top of the side allowance in a straight horizontal line at the same level as the pinned dart, removing the excess flap which remains above the deck level.

Take the lip section off the chair. Trim the fabric above the lip/deck curve to ½ inch above the chalk line. Later, you'll sew the side allowance to the lip/deck curve to fit around the lip's spring edge and into the crevice between the lip and the inside arm.

Non-spring-edge lips. Only a T-shaped non-spring-edge lip needs to be fitted before upholstering. A rectangular non-spring-edge lip is fitted only when you put it on your furniture.

Fit a T-shaped non-spring-edge lip as you would a T-shaped spring-edge lip (see page 54), with one difference. When you remove the lip outer-cover section from the chair, trim the lip/deck curve seam allowance to two inches above the lip/deck curve's chalk line, instead of to a ½ inch. You'll need these two inches later for tacking.

Inside wing. Place the inside-wing outer-cover section over the inside surface of the wing on your furniture, aligning the section so that the correct allowances extend past all the edges. Slide the section's back edge into the crevice between the inside back and the inside wing; pin the section's front edge at the top and bottom. With sharpened chalk, trace the inside wing's bottom edge. If you are unable to trace the inside wing's bottom edge all the way to the wing's back edge (since the back edge will be hidden by the inside back), you can continue the traced edge to the section's back edge by estimate. Remove the section from the furniture and place it on a flat surface; complete and refine the chalk line.

Trim the wing's bottom allowance to a ½ inch below the chalk line. Later, you'll sew welt along this edge.

Wing-chair wrap-around boxed arms. Center the boxing outer-cover section on the arm top so that it has the correct allowances on all sides. To make the boxing lie flat where the inside wing joins the arm top, you'll need to make a long cut from the boxing's rear to within one inch of the inside wing's front edge (see illustration 23). Pin the boxing in place. Starting where the inside arm meets the inside back and the inside wing, and ending where the inside arm meets the outside arm, trace the arm top's curved edge with sharpened chalk. Remove

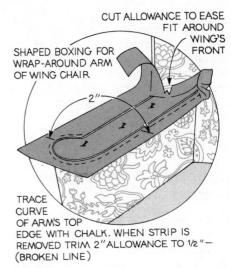

CUT ALLOWANCE TO EASE FIT AROUND WING'S FRONT

SHAPED BOXING FOR WRAP-AROUND ARM OF WING CHAIR

2"

TRACE CURVE OF ARM'S TOP EDGE WITH CHALK. WHEN STRIP IS REMOVED TRIM 2" ALLOWANCE TO ½"— (BROKEN LINE)

ill. 23

the section from the chair; refine the chalk line and cut around the curve, leaving a ½-inch seam allowance. As you continue to trim along the outside edge of the arm section, widen the seam allowance past the point where the chalk line ends, to become a 2-inch tacking allowance.

Attached-cushion ottoman. Cut the ottoman's cushion faces and boxing from your bolt of fabric, following the centering and matching techniques explained on page 39, and applying the instructions for a cushion's front boxing to your ottoman cushion's side boxing. To shape the ottoman's cushion faces further, see pages 87–88.

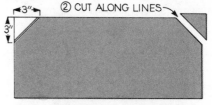

① MEASURE AND DRAW DIAGONAL LINES
② CUT ALONG LINES

3"

3"

FITTING ATTACHED-CUSHION OTTOMAN SIDE AND END PANELS

ill. 24

The outer-cover sections for the ottoman's side and end panels will be sewn eventually to the bottom cushion face. To shape these sections, preparatory to sewing them, measure three inches down from the top corners of each panel, along the right and left edges, and mark. Also measure three inches in from the top corners toward the center of the top edge of each panel, and mark. Join the two marked points at each corner with a diagonal line. Cut along these lines.

Keeping cut cover sections in order

It's helpful to have all parts of an outer-cover section—the section itself, plus any boxing, welt, or stretchers to be attached to it—rolled together, to keep them organized and to prevent creasing, before you sit down to sew.

Before rolling the parts together, make sure you've marked each part completely: top, front, stretcher, and seam allowance lines—whatever is needed to know exactly how to put the section together.

If a section is going to have welt, measure welt strips to fit it (see illustration 25). Note, however, that when measuring welt for a T-shaped inside back, you must extend the welt strip below the back's bottom edge on both sides of the inside back. Use any long, unspliced welt strips for the most visible parts of each section, such as the top and sides of a fully upholstered armchair's inside back.

MEASURING WELT TO FIT INSIDE BACK

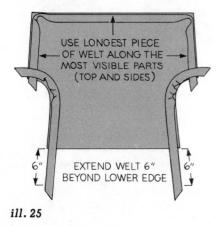

USE LONGEST PIECE OF WELT ALONG THE MOST VISIBLE PARTS (TOP AND SIDES)

6"   EXTEND WELT 6"   6"
     BEYOND LOWER EDGE

ill. 25

Place any welt, boxing, and stretchers on the main section's right side and roll them up loosely in the main section; set aside. If you can't see a section's label after rolling, chalk it on the outside (which will be the fabric's wrong side) or pin a paper label on it.

Only three sections of the fully upholstered armchair are rolled together with other pieces: the inside back with its boxing pieces, stretchers, and welt strips; the front border with its welt strip; and the deck cushion faces with welt strips, front boxing, and zipper boxings. You'll tack welt onto the remaining sections after they are put on the chair.

Machine-sewing parts of outer cover

Most of the sewing involved in upholstery is done by hand as you're putting the outer cover on (see pages 63–95). But if your furniture sports one or more cushions, a skirt, boxing fitted to its inside back or inside arms, or edges rimmed with welt, you'll need to sew some outer-cover sections by machine. (For information on loose cushions and skirts, see pages 87–95.)

A home sewing machine works fine for sewing light and medium-weight fabrics. To make cushions and double welt with heavy-weight fabrics, however, you'll need an industrial-grade machine. You may be able to use one in an upholstery shop for a fee, or hire a professional upholsterer to do your sewing.

Setting up to sew

Everything you need to prepare for the machine-sewing segment of your reupholstering process—tools, types of seams, techniques for sewing sections to fit—appears on the following pages.

Tools you'll need. Except for some heavy-weight thread and a sewing-machine needle of the proper size, you probably won't have to buy any tools to do your machine-sewing.

You'll need a zipper foot (standard with most modern machines) for putting zippers in cushion boxings, making welt, and sewing welt to outer-cover sections.

Use a #16 or #100 needle for light and medium-weight fabrics, and a #18 or #110 needle for heavy-weight ones.

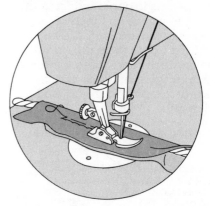

USE A ZIPPER FOOT TO MAKE WELT

ill. 26

T-pins or standard dressmaker's pins are needed to hold matched or fitted sections in place as you sew.

You can use upholstery shears as you sew, but small scissors are easier to handle when clipping threads or snipping welt seam allowance to make it go around a corner smoothly.

Keep a seam ripper handy, in case you make a mistake.

Seams you'll use. You do all upholstery sewing with a standard straight stitch. Sew ½-inch-wide seams throughout, unless directed otherwise; backstitch the beginning and end of all seams to lock the ends of the seams in place.

When working with loosely woven fabrics or with synthetic fabrics that have backing, line the seams with ¾-inch-wide strips of muslin or other tightly woven cotton, aligned on the wrong side of the outer-cover fabric, raw edges together. Also line bias

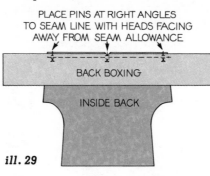

REINFORCE DIAGONAL SEAM WITH 3/4" FABRIC STRIP

BIAS

ill. 27

seams (seams that run diagonally, at a 45° angle to your fabric's yarns), to prevent the thread from breaking when the seam is under stress.

To join two scraps of fabric together to make a stretcher, overlap their edges by ½ inch, placing the wrong side of the top piece over the right side of the bottom piece, and stitch them together. To join a stretcher to a cover section, sew a standard seam, then top-stitch it by folding the seam allowances toward the stretcher and sewing them down with another seam, ¼ inch from the first seam line. This top-stitching is important—it strengthens the seam so that it can bear the strain of pulling and tugging while reupholstering.

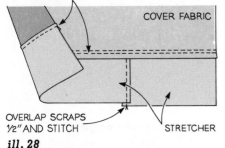

TO JOIN STRETCHER TO COVER FABRIC, SEW SEAM AND TOP-STITCH ¼" BELOW SEAM

COVER FABRIC

OVERLAP SCRAPS ½" AND STITCH   STRETCHER

ill. 28

Section-fitting techniques. Here are some techniques used by professionals to insure the proper fitting of two cover sections as they're sewn together.

Step 1: Fold sections in half along length. Cut a notch in top of each fold to mark center of edges to be matched and sewn together.

Step 2: Matching notches and aligning edges, place right sides of the two sections together

and secure with two or three pins. Place pins at right angles to the future seam line, with their heads away from seam allowance.

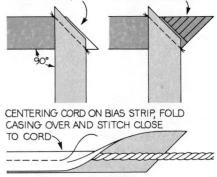

PLACE PINS AT RIGHT ANGLES TO SEAM LINE WITH HEADS FACING AWAY FROM SEAM ALLOWANCE

BACK BOXING

INSIDE BACK

ill. 29

Step 3: When sewing boxings to cover sections with dominant motifs, check frequently to be sure the motifs remain properly matched.

Step 4: Unless you are experienced in matching dominant motifs, sew two matched sections together, beginning first at seam's most visible part. For example, when joining a back-boxing section to an inside back, first sew the seam at the top, then those at the sides of the inside back.

Step 5: As you sew two sections together, pull back gently on bottom section to keep sections properly aligned.

Welt: Sewing it and sewing with it

The term "welt" generally refers to single welt. You either sew single welt to the outer-cover sections, such as inside backs and cushions, or you tack it to the frame to line the furniture's outside edges. Double welt, most often used in place of gimp, is glued over outer-cover sections at exposed wood edges.

Set your sewing machine for the longest possible stitch and attach the zipper foot. Sewing with the zipper foot, you can make single welt out of any weight of fabric and double welt out of light-weight and some medium-weight fabrics.

Sewing single welt. Join bias strips together, end to end, to make a continuous length of bias

casing for welt only when you are sewing together all the parts of the section to which the welt will be attached.

With right sides together, position the ends of two bias strips at right angles to each other, offset so their points protrude slightly (see illustration 30), and join them with a ¼-inch seam; press the seam open. Continue to join bias strips together until the total casing length will fit all the way around the perimeter of the section requiring welt.

HOW TO MAKE SINGLE WELT

OVERLAP BIAS ENDS AT 90° ANGLE–STITCH AND TRIM TO ¼"   IF BIAS ENDS DON'T MATCH, TRIM AWAY TRIANGULAR PIECE

90°

CENTERING CORD ON BIAS STRIP, FOLD CASING OVER AND STITCH CLOSE TO CORD

ill. 30

Lay the cord along the center of your bias casing's wrong side. Let the cord extend six inches past each end of the casing, to compensate for any stretch in the bias casing and to keep the cord from disappearing into the casing when you sew the welt to an outer-cover section.

Aligning its raw edges, fold the casing over the cord. Sew a seam down the length of the casing, close to—but not crowding—the cord. With one hand in front and one hand in back of the sewing-machine needle, gently stretch the bias casing as you sew. The stretching helps the welt to lie smoothly in the cover seams and around edges.

Later, if you're sewing the welt to an outer-cover section, you'll hide the welt seam by stitching even closer to the cord. If you're tacking the welt to the furniture's frame, the outer-cover sections will hide the welt seam (see page 89).

Sewing with single welt. To sew single welt to an outer-cover section, place it on the right side of the section, align the raw edges of both welt and outer-cover section, and sew tightly against, but not through, the welt's cord, inside the welt seam.

To make welt turn a corner as you attach it to an outer-cover section, make three diagonal cuts into the welt seam allowance, *almost* to the seam's stitching. Make one cut right at the corner and one a ½ inch to each side of the corner cut.

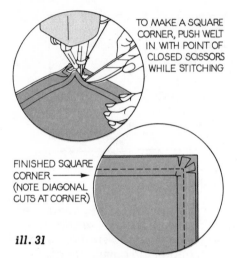

TO MAKE A SQUARE CORNER, PUSH WELT IN WITH POINT OF CLOSED SCISSORS WHILE STITCHING

FINISHED SQUARE CORNER → (NOTE DIAGONAL CUTS AT CORNER)

ill. 31

Leaving the machine's needle lowered through the fabric to anchor it, rotate the section 90°, together with the welt, stitching tightly against the welt cord as you round the corner. Before you continue to sew the seam on the new side, prod the welt gently at the corner with the points of a closed pair of scissors to make the corner square instead of rounded. A tightly sewn square corner looks good and holds its shape well.

Sewing double welt. Place two equal lengths of cord, side by side, on the wrong side of the bias casing near the right-hand edge. Fold the casing's right-hand edge

over both cords, just to the inner (second) cord's outer edge. Tightly roll the folded casing and cords carefully over once, toward the left, so that they still lie on the casing's wrong side.

HOW TO MAKE DOUBLE WELT

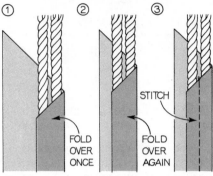

① ② ③

STITCH

FOLD OVER ONCE

FOLD OVER AGAIN

ill. 32

Holding the rolled cords and casing in place, slide the welt under the zipper foot, positioning the needle between the two cords. Start sewing a ½ inch from the end, backstitch, then continue the seam.

You'll have to hold the casing and cords in place throughout, checking occasionally to see that your stitching is catching the casing's inner edge, but not the cords (see illustration 32). This inner edge slides out of place if you're not careful, especially when the casing is velvet or some other slippery fabric.

When you are ready to use the welt, trim off the seam allowance to within ⅛ inch of the welt seam's stitching.

If your fabric is too heavy to make into double welt on your home sewing machine and you need only a small quantity of this kind of welt, use the zipper foot to make single welt near one edge of the welt casing. Trim the narrower seam allowance of the casing to ¼ inch; place another cord alongside the single welt, fold the casing over again, and sew it by hand to enclose the second cord.

Order of sewing

Sew the outer-cover sections in the order you'll put them on the furniture: the seat (including both lip and decking), then the front

border, inside arms, inside wings (if any), inside back, and any welt that is to be tacked to the furniture. You'll hand-sew the outside arms and outside back right on furniture.

Seat. Spring-edge lips and T-shaped non-spring-edge lips are fitted and sewn before you attach them to the decking. Sewing instructions for fitted lips follow. To attach a lip section to the decking, first fold the decking in half along its length; notch the center of its front edge. The notched center enables you to position the lip section correctly over the decking before you sew them together.

Rectangular spring-edge lip. Sew each cut-out corner of the lip together, leaving a ½-inch seam allowance. Right sides together, match the center notches of the lip and decking and pin them at the notches and lip seams; join them with a ½-inch seam.

½" SEAM JOINING EDGE OF LIP AND DECKING

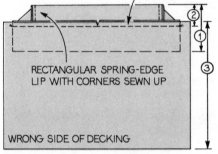

RECTANGULAR SPRING-EDGE LIP WITH CORNERS SEWN UP

WRONG SIDE OF DECKING

① ②
①
③

①VERTICAL PART OF LIP
②HORIZONTAL PART OF LIP   ③DECKING

ill. 33

T-shaped spring-edge lip. Sew the lip's edge dart, working from the front of the lip toward the back. Leave the needle lowered through the fabric to anchor it. Align the raw edges of the side allowance and the lip/deck curve, right sides together. Rotating the sections, sew a ½-inch seam around the curve to the curve's end. Repeat on the lip's other side.

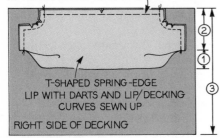

½" SEAM JOINING EDGE OF LIP AND DECKING

T-SHAPED SPRING-EDGE LIP WITH DARTS AND LIP/DECKING CURVES SEWN UP

RIGHT SIDE OF DECKING

① VERTICAL PART OF LIP
② HORIZONTAL PART OF LIP ③ DECKING

ill. 34

Place the lip on the decking at the decking's front edge, right sides together. Match the center notches; pin the sections together at the notches and lip seams; join them with a ½-inch seam.

Rectangular non-spring-edge lip. Place the lip section on the decking at the decking's front edge, right sides together. Match the center notches and pin the two sections together. Join them with a ½-inch seam.

RECTANGULAR NON-SPRING-EDGE LIP

½" SEAM

LIP

DECKING

RIGHT SIDE OF DECKING

ill. 35

T-shaped non-spring-edge lip. Sew the lip's edge darts, working from the lip's front toward its back. Place the lip on the decking at the decking's front edge, right sides together. Match the center

notches; pin the sections together, and join them with a ½-inch seam.

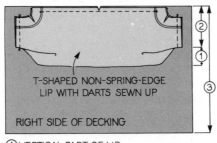

½" SEAM JOINING EDGE OF LIP AND DECKING

T-SHAPED NON-SPRING-EDGE LIP WITH DARTS SEWN UP

RIGHT SIDE OF DECKING

① VERTICAL PART OF LIP
② HORIZONTAL PART OF LIP ③ DECKING

ill. 36

Front border. If you're adding welt to your outer cover, place a length of welt on the front border's right side, aligning it with the border's top edge. Join the welt and border along the welt seam line.

Inside wing. Align the raw edge of the welt seam allowance with the inside-wing outer-cover section's raw bottom edge on the fabric's right side. Sew the welt to the section along the the welt seam line. Let the welt ends extend four inches past the back and front edges of the inside-wing section. These dangling ends are used to pull the inside-wing outer-cover section's bottom taut over the inside arm as you upholster.

Wing-chair wrap-around boxed arms. Align the raw edges of the welt and the boxing seam allowance. Sew the welt to the boxing's shaped edge, starting where the boxing meets the inside back

WRAP-AROUND BOXED ARM FOR WING CHAIR WITH BOXING SEWN TO INSIDE ARM

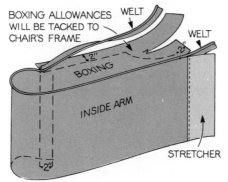

BOXING ALLOWANCES WILL BE TACKED TO CHAIR'S FRAME

WELT

WELT

BOXING

12"

2"

INSIDE ARM

STRETCHER

2"

ill. 37

and ending at the point where the inside arm will meet the outside arm. Leave enough welt dangling to reach the back of the outside arm at its top.

Sew the boxing to the inside arm's top edge, right sides together. Attach a stretcher to the inside arm's back edge. The arm's bottom edge needs no stretcher as the inside-arm fabric section itself reaches down to the lip's bottom and thus has enough length for tacking.

T-shaped inside back. Sew a T-shaped inside back, using the following steps.

Step 1: Sew a stretcher to bottom edge of inside back.

Step 2: Piece bias strips together for welt, taking care to place the longest strip in the middle so that the welt on inside back's top edge shows no seams. Finish welt (see page 53).

Step 3: Fold inside-back section along its length and notch center of its top edge.

Step 4: Sew welt around inside back's sides and top in a continuous length. Begin by placing welt so that one end extends six inches below inside back's bottom edge (excluding stretcher). Align

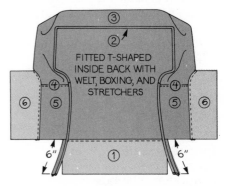

③
②
FITTED T-SHAPED INSIDE BACK WITH WELT, BOXING, AND STRETCHERS
④ ④
⑥ ⑤   ⑤ ⑥
6" ① 6"

① SEW STRETCHER TO BOTTOM OF INSIDE BACK
② SEW WELT TO INSIDE BACK'S TOP AND SIDES, LEAVING 6" HANGING FREE AT EACH END
③ JOIN VISABLE BACK BOXING TO INSIDE BACK
④ JOIN HIDDEN BACK BOXING PIECES TO VISIBLE BACK BOXING
⑤ ATTACH HIDDEN BACK BOXING PIECES AT SIDES
⑥ SEW STRETCHERS TO BOXING BELOW T'S BOTTOM CORNERS

ill. 38

raw edges of welt seam allowance and inside-back section's seam allowance. Sew welt in place as you align it around inside back's edges. Let welt's other end extend six inches past inside back's bottom edge at opposite side when you finish seam. You'll use the dangling welt ends to pull cover snug against inside back when upholstering.

Step 5: Fold visible back boxing in half along its length and notch center of its bottom edge.

Step 6: Match center notches of inside back's top edge and boxing's bottom edge. Pin sections together at center and at top corners.

Step 7: If back-boxing motifs must match the ones on inside back, join boxing in two separate seams. First, sew boxing to inside back's top, backstitching at each end. Then sew boxing to both inside-back sides, starting from below curve and working up to top corner of each side. Snip boxing seam allowance to make it turn corner at top of curve and top of inside back, as you would a welt seam allowance. Let side seams overlap top seam by two inches before backstitching.

Step 8: Sew hidden-back-boxing pieces to both sides of inside back with a ½-inch seam. Sew hidden-back-boxing pieces to the visible-back-boxing sections on both sides with a ½-inch seam.

Step 9: Sew stretchers to sides of hidden back boxing below the T's lower corners.

Attached-cushion ottoman. The side and end panels, sewn together, form the base cover of an attached-cushion ottoman. You attach the base cover to the bottom cushion face before finishing the cushion.

Sew the diagonally cut tops of the side and end panels together, as shown in illustration 39. Line the seams with ½-inch strips of muslin aligned on the fabric's wrong side; press the seam allowances open. Chalk a ½-inch seam line all around the base cover's rectangular or square top edge.

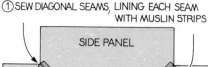

SEWING ATTACHED-CUSHION OTTOMAN'S BASE COVER

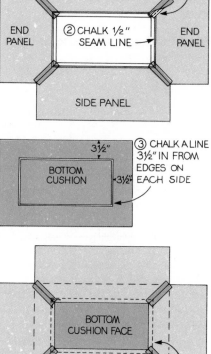

① SEW DIAGONAL SEAMS, LINING EACH SEAM WITH MUSLIN STRIPS

SIDE PANEL

END PANEL   ② CHALK ½" SEAM LINE   END PANEL

SIDE PANEL

3½"   ③ CHALK A LINE 3½" IN FROM EDGES ON EACH SIDE

BOTTOM CUSHION   3½"

BOTTOM CUSHION FACE

BASE COVER

④ ALIGN BASE COVER'S TOP EDGES WITH CUSHION FACE'S CHALK LINE THEN STITCH ALONG ½" SEAM LINE

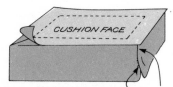

CUSHION FACE

⑤ SEW VERTICAL SEAMS OF BASE-COVER PANELS
ill. 39

On the right side of the bottom cushion face, chalk a rectangle (or square, if your cushion is square) with its sides 3½ inches in from each edge.

Place the base cover over the bottom cushion face, right sides together. Align the base cover's top edges with the chalked rectangle or square on the bottom cushion face. Pin at all four corners.

Attach the base cover to the cushion face with a ½-inch seam all around the base cover's top edges. Finally, sew the base cover panels together at their bottom side edges.

To finish sewing the cushion, follow the instructions on page 90. Stuff the cushion according to the instructions on page 91.

Attached-cushion ottoman border. If your fabric is vertically run, sew the side edges of the border pieces together to make one long width of fabric (don't join the final free side edges to make a circle). If your fabric is railroaded, you will already have been able to cut the whole border out in one continuous width.

Double-check the border's width by wrapping it around the ottoman's base at border height; fold the border's free side edges under at a corner so the edges of the folds meet. Pin each fold at its top; remove the border from the ottoman and press the folds with an iron. Pin the free side edges together with the fold marks joined; sew a seam along the fold marks (the border will now form a circle). Press the seam open.

Place a welt end about six inches from a border seam along a border end piece's top edge; aligning the welt's seam allowance with the border's top edge. Leaving three inches unattached at the welt's end, sew the welt to the border's top edge until you're within three inches of your starting point. Join the welt ends as explained on page 90. Turn the border wrong side up; press the welt and border seam allowances so the welt rims the border's top edge.

Stripping
Old Fabric

If you've never stripped fabric from a chair or sofa, you may be startled by the seeming complexity of the inside of a piece of upholstered furniture. But if you follow the techniques suggested in this section, you should be able to sort out your furniture's components and ready it for its new cover without much strain.

A fully upholstered armchair was chosen as this book's star, on which to demonstrate the art of stripping, and most other reupholstering operations. It is about as orthodox a piece of furniture as you can find, and so serves as a good basic example of upholstering techniques.

Begin by examining, in detail, the external features of this chair, and its insides (see illustrations 1 and 2). It has a square deck cushion (not T-shaped or round in the front), arms that come all the way to its front, back boxing (top and shoulders area between the inside and outside back), and a spring-edge lip. Its springs are of the coil variety. Its frame not only makes the chair sturdy, but also provides a hitching post for fabric.

Your own piece could easily differ from this fully upholstered armchair. Perhaps the old fabric is stapled rather than tacked, or perhaps it extends into a skirt around the legs. You may have a settee for which zigzag springs

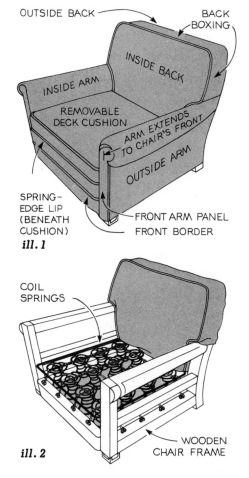

OUTSIDE BACK — BACK BOXING
INSIDE BACK
INSIDE ARM
REMOVABLE DECK CUSHION
ARM EXTENDS TO CHAIR'S FRONT
OUTSIDE ARM
SPRING-EDGE LIP (BENEATH CUSHION)
FRONT ARM PANEL
FRONT BORDER
ill. 1

COIL SPRINGS
WOODEN CHAIR FRAME
ill. 2

provide the bounce, or a chair or sofa with a T-shaped deck. Still, most of the stripping techniques that work for this chair will work for your furniture as well. Where variations on the directions are necessary to suit your furniture piece, we will provide them.

Whichever method you use to loosen your old cover and its stretchers, take your time. Going slowly acquaints you with the way the furniture is put together, especially how and where the

various fabric sections are attached. With such knowledge, you can minimize mistakes when attaching the new cover.

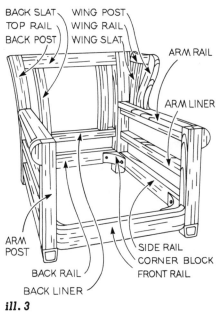

BACK SLAT
TOP RAIL
BACK POST
WING POST
WING RAIL
WING SLAT
ARM RAIL
ARM LINER
ARM POST
BACK RAIL
BACK LINER
SIDE RAIL
CORNER BLOCK
FRONT RAIL
ill. 3

As you strip, loosen no more fabric than you have to. Your old chaise longue, for instance, may boast a muslin undercover. The chances are that, with care, you can leave the undercover intact, saving yourself work when the time comes to secure the new cover.

It's important to leave the old inside back, inside arms, and decking in place after you remove almost all their tacks or staples. Not only does the old fabric keep loose padding out of your way while you're retacking a new section; it also helps you remember how the inside sections fit together. You need not leave outside pieces in place because the furniture's frame gives you all the outside template you require.

Fabric stripping often yields unsought results. The older your piece, the more likely you will be to discover coins, rings, buttons, and other treasures that have slipped into cracks over the years.

Stripping preparation

Stripping furniture is dusty work. Wear old clothes and lay in a plentiful supply of tissues, in case of sneezes. Keep tools handy in a sturdy apron pocket or on a nearby bench.

Your reupholstering project may span several months of weekends, so you should try to find a work place, such as a basement or garage, where you can leave the chair or sofa undisturbed. You'll also want to allow enough space to walk around and work on all sides of the furniture.

You may wish to cover the floor with tarpaulins or old sheets, to protect it from debris and the tacks or staples you pry loose. Stepped-on tacks are most easily removed from thick crepe-soled shoes; they bite deep into tennis shoes, and can badly fray leather soles.

You can strip small items—an ottoman, a dining room chair—on a tabletop. Heavier items can rest on the floor, if you don't mind stooping while working. But you can save your back by building a pair of upholsterer's horses to support your furniture at a more comfortable height; page 62 shows you how.

Before you begin stripping, survey the furniture's frame for loose joints and visible breaks. As you peel away fabric you may discover additional structural problems; these should be repaired before reupholstering begins (see page 32).

Fabric stripping techniques

Two basic methods exist for peeling fabric from furniture. You'll probably use both before you're through.

Yanking fabric free with pliers takes the least amount of time. Use this method when tacks or staples are sunk so deeply into the frame that prying them out without tearing the fabric proves difficult. Pliers are also handy for freeing welt, or stretchers tacked on top of burlap or webbing.

PULL WELT FREE WITH PLIERS

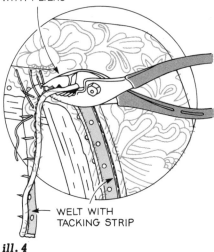
WELT WITH TACKING STRIP

ill. 4

Though a professional upholsterer wields pliers with the abandon of a violinist wielding a bow, you may wish to proceed with more caution. It is to the beginner's advantage to keep the old outer-cover sections intact, as they may help in visualizing how to put the new cover on. Pliers shred the old fabric, besides sending tacks flying.

The slower, more common method of freeing fabric involves a chisel or claw tool, and a tack hammer or rubber mallet. The forked claw tool keeps tacks or

decorative nails straighter than the chisel does, in case you wish to reuse them. The chisel, though, is less likely to chew up fabric.

If you tap the claw tool or chisel with a tack hammer, use the hammer's side; the ends tend to glance off the tool's end and bruise your hands. Substituting a rubber mallet for the tack hammer lets you deal with thuds rather than a hammer's loud clanks. (When not using the tack hammer, keep its head's smaller end away from metal, in order to preserve its magnetism.)

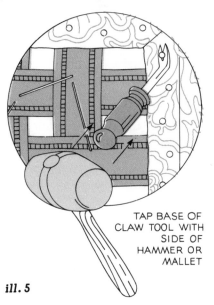
TAP BASE OF CLAW TOOL WITH SIDE OF HAMMER OR MALLET

ill. 5

Whichever tools you choose for tack removal, try to approach the tacks with—rather than against—the grain of the wood. This helps prevent splintering. You can decrease gouging by hitting the angled tool on its handle end only until you drive its metal tip beneath the tack head. Then push the tool's handle end toward the chair frame with your free hand while you hit its handle's side with the hammer or mallet; this lifts the tack out gently.

The more old tacks you can remove from the frame, the greater choice of surface you have for driving new tacks in, and the flatter your new fabric surface will be.

When wood immediately underlies the fabric you wish to remove, place your claw tool or chisel between the tack head and the cloth, thus cushioning the frame against blows. When one fabric layer lies atop another, and you wish to remove both, free the top layer first by placing your tool underneath it.

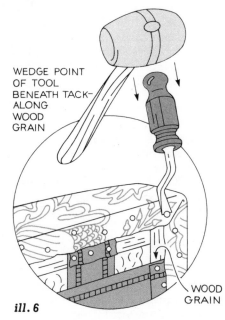

WEDGE POINT OF TOOL BENEATH TACK ALONG WOOD GRAIN

WOOD GRAIN

ill. 6

By stripping your chair or sofa in the reverse order in which it was originally upholstered, you can easily and thoroughly prepare to apply its new cover. Writing down and numbering the sequence of layers you strip will aid your memory, as will taking photographs or making drawings of each layer. As you remove each fabric section, pin to it a scrap of paper bearing an abbreviation of the section's name, and set the section aside. The more paraphernalia—tacks, tacking strips, twine, padding— you can leave intact with each section, the better visual reference it offers when you begin to attach new material.

Step by step: Stripping a fully upholstered armchair

1 Place chair upright on upholsterer's horses.

2 If chair has a skirt, detach it now. Probably the skirt assembly (including illusory pleat backdrops and welt) is tacked or stapled through underlying fabric to chair's wooden rails. If skirt attaches at a point higher or lower than rails, it will be sewn to underlying fabric. In either case, cut through skirt, possible cardboard tacking strip, and welt in any spot other than at an illusory pleat. Yank skirt assembly free with pliers. Skirts sewn to underlying fabric require you to sever twine while you pull the skirt free.

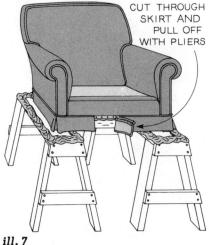

CUT THROUGH SKIRT AND PULL OFF WITH PLIERS

ill. 7

3 Remove tacks holding dustcatcher, lift dustcatcher free, and set aside. (If staples replace tacks, see page 61.) Note how its edges are probably doubled under for extra holding strength.

Are there holes or worn areas in crisscrossed webbing underneath? Does webbing "give" a lot when you tug it? Then you'll have to reinforce or replace it later. Pages 97–99 show you how.

SAGGING WEBBING

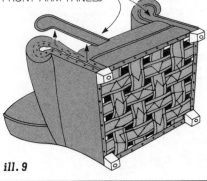

ill. 8 REMOVE TACKS FROM DUSTCATCHER

Look at the twine that secures coil spring bottoms to webbing. If this twine has been severed, you'll eventually have to re-anchor springs as shown starting on page 100. Don't re-anchor now.

4 Remove tacks from bottom edges of outside back, outside arms, and front border. Do not remove larger tacks holding webbing to back posts unless you must remove tacks in order to free outer-cover edges.

5 Lay chair on its back on the floor.

6 With claw tool or chisel, pry off two front arm panels; set these aside.

PRY OFF BOTH FRONT ARM PANELS

ill. 9

7 Remove tacks from fabric edges on arm fronts, previously hidden by front arm panels. Note how inside arm fabric is pleated at its curved front top in order to produce a snug fit. Claw tool is easiest to use in yanking out tacks holding pleats in place.

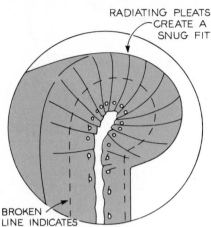

RADIATING PLEATS CREATE A SNUG FIT

BROKEN LINE INDICATES POSITION OF REMOVED FRONT PANEL
ill. 10

As you work, you'll begin to see the felted cotton that serves as padding beneath most cover sections and the wood frame. You may also glimpse, especially on the inside arms of older chairs, lightweight muslin or other fabric stretched beneath the padding. This undercover was at one time used to smooth interior stuffing; take care not to loosen its tacks. If

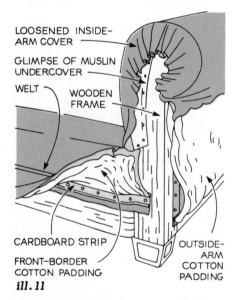

LOOSENED INSIDE-ARM COVER

GLIMPSE OF MUSLIN UNDERCOVER

WELT

WOODEN FRAME

CARDBOARD STRIP

FRONT-BORDER COTTON PADDING
ill. 11

OUTSIDE-ARM COTTON PADDING

you later discover you must remove the undercover, it need not be replaced.

8 Lift bottom of front border. Note padding and ½-inch cardboard strip beneath welt at top. When prying border's top loose, place chisel or claw tool beneath welt. Include tacks and remains of cardboard strip—in place, if possible—when you set border aside, as they will help you see how to install new border.

9 Untack front of lip.

10 Place chair upright on upholsterer's horses.

11 Progressing from bottom to top, cut twine by which outside back is sewn to two outside arms and back boxing. Leave twine remnants attached to arm and back-boxing fabric to help you see how to resew.

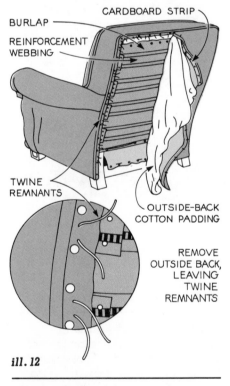

CARDBOARD STRIP

BURLAP

REINFORCEMENT WEBBING

TWINE REMNANTS

OUTSIDE-BACK COTTON PADDING

REMOVE OUTSIDE BACK, LEAVING TWINE REMNANTS

ill. 12

12 Lift outside back; note cardboard strip and tacks anchoring its top. Loosen tacks by placing tool between outside back and fabric underneath. Remove as a unit the outside back, padding, and cardboard strip; label *OB*, and set aside.

13 Twine sewn through outside-back burlap stretched across frame indicates chair has coil springs. Remove tacks only from burlap's sides along back posts (do not loosen at bottom or top). You will have to remove some of the webbing at the sides as well.

Your chair may have back slats—extra frame members running vertically from top rail to back liner, parallel to back posts. If so, you'll probably find another layer of burlap outside the webbing, tacked at top to top rail, at bottom to back liner, and at sides to back slats. Remove the outside layer of burlap completely; you will be able to complete Step 14 without removing inner burlap's sides—tacked to back slats— at all.

14 Gently push sides of burlap aside to see where inside back/back boxing and inside-arm stretchers are tacked to back posts. (If your chair has back slats, the inside-back and inside-arm stretchers will already be visible in gap between slats and posts.) Carefully prod and remove all but a few tacks keeping inside-back and inside-arm stretchers attached to frame. Also carefully prod and remove all but a few tacks holding decking and inside-back stretchers to back rail, below burlap's bottom edge.

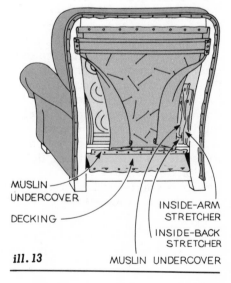

MUSLIN UNDERCOVER

DECKING

INSIDE-ARM STRETCHER

INSIDE-BACK STRETCHER

MUSLIN UNDERCOVER

ill. 13

15 Untack welt that runs up back post, around top rail, and down other back post. Set aside.

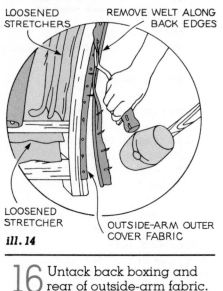

LOOSENED STRETCHERS

REMOVE WELT ALONG BACK EDGES

LOOSENED STRETCHER

OUTSIDE-ARM OUTER COVER FABRIC

ill. 14

16 Untack back boxing and rear of outside-arm fabric.

17 Remove all but two tacks of the inside-back outer cover at its top and sides; leave on chair.

18 Set chair on its side on the floor. Loosen outside arm's top by placing chisel beneath top layer of fabric to raise each tack. Remove as a unit the outside arm, padding, and cardboard strip; label *OA*, and set aside.

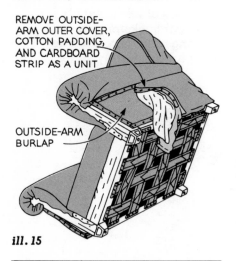

REMOVE OUTSIDE-ARM OUTER COVER, COTTON PADDING, AND CARDBOARD STRIP AS A UNIT

OUTSIDE-ARM BURLAP

ill. 15

19 Remove outside-arm burlap, label it *OAB*, and set aside.

20 Follow stretcher directions in Step 14 to loosen remaining inside-arm stretchers and decking still tacked to frame. If deck stuffing and inside-arm stuffing are protected by an undercover, do not remove undercover tacks.

21 Remove all but two tacks that secure inside arm's top, including any tacks holding inside arm's rear to back post. The two remaining tacks will hold outer cover and padding in place until you're ready to re-cover.

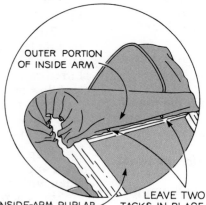

OUTER PORTION OF INSIDE ARM

INSIDE-ARM BURLAP

LEAVE TWO TACKS IN PLACE

ill. 16

22 Repeat Steps 18–21 on second outside arm.

All outside covers are now untacked. This is the time to decide whether you can start putting the new cover on (see next chapter) or must first attend to your furniture's insides (pages 96–110).

Fabric-stripping variations

Even if your furniture does not exactly resemble the fully upholstered armchair shown on page 57, read through the preceding stripping steps before perusing the following variations. You'll find that much of the basic information that applies to the armchair applies to your piece as well.

Less expensive furniture. As you begin to strip less expensive furniture, you may discover that cardboard is substituted for burlap, or that the outside-arm and

outside-back cavities are protected by nothing but outer-cover fabric. Don't despair; you can add burlap and cotton padding when reupholstering. Because you won't reuse cardboard, rip it away as fast as you wish, and discard it.

Staples. Because staples cost less than tacks and are faster to apply, inexpensive pieces and even reupholstered expensive pieces often exhibit more staples than tacks, securing the burlap or cardboard, the padding, and the fabric to the frame.

Slip the corner of your claw tool or chisel under the staple to lift it. The staple may pop out of the frame completely, or you may have to yank it free with pliers. Unfortunately, a staple's two prongs often pierce the frame along the grain. This means you must dig across the grain to get under the staple, increasing the chances that you'll gouge or splinter the wood. Your best hedge against such damage is to worm your tool underneath the staple's bridge at as slight an angle as you can muster.

Wings. Think of a chair's wings as budding back-height arms that changed their minds. Remove the outside-wing outer cover, along with possible attendant padding and welt, after you pull off the outside back and outside arm (Steps 10–19); label it *OW*, and set aside. Untack enough of the underlying burlap or webbing to be able to reach the inside-wing outer cover wedged between the back post and back slat (see frame diagram on page 57). Pry the cover free and leave it in position. Remove all but three tacks from the inside-wing perimeter; these hold the padding in place until you're ready to re-cover.

Zigzag springs. You may find zigzag springs attached to the burlap underlying the inside back, but they sit too far in to be attached to burlap underlying the outside back. This means that in Step 14, you can remove the outside-back burlap completely before loosening the stretchers.

HOW TO MAKE UPHOLSTERER'S HORSES

Two upholsterer's horses facilitate the handling of your furniture during your reupholstery project. By lifting the furniture off the floor, the horses make it approachable from all angles, saving you considerable frustration, not to mention back strain. The padded troughs on top of the horses prevent your furniture from sliding off.

If you ask the lumberyard to cut your wood, a hammer is the only tool you'll need to construct your own pair of horses. Present the lumberyard with the following measurements; they specify enough wood for two horses:

- Two 36" lengths of 2 by 4 fir (for the saddles)
- Four 36" lengths of 1 by 4 fir (for the side braces)
- Eight 28" lengths of 1 by 4 fir (for the legs—you may choose lengths from 24" to 36" depending on which height is most convenient for you.)
- Four 13½" lengths of 1 by 4 fir (for the lower cross braces)
- Four 7½" lengths of 1 by 4 fir (for the upper cross braces)
- Four 36" lengths of 1 by 3 fir (for the side rails)
- Four 7½" lengths of 1 by 3 fir (for the end rails)

In addition, you'll need:

- One ½ pound of 6-penny (2") common nails
- One 3-ounce box of #10 (⅝") carpet tacks
- Two pieces of carpeting or heavy upholstery fabric, each 40 inches long and 17 inches wide

All joints eventually require two nails, except where the legs join the saddle; these need three. At all joints other than leg/saddle joints, wait to drive any nails all the way in until you've placed all of them halfway in. Step-by-step instructions for a single horse follow. Two pairs of hands simplify the job of fixing the horse's legs at the proper angles (Steps 1-4):

Step 1: Nail two 28" legs to either side of one end of a saddle, making sure leg tops lie flush with saddle top.

Step 2: Turn saddle so its free end points skyward. Lay a 7½" upper cross brace across legs, abutting saddle bottom.

Step 3: Pry legs apart until 7½" brace's bottom just reaches from one leg's outside

surface to the other's. Drive a single nail through brace near brace's bottom, halfway into each leg.

Step 4: Repeat Steps 1 through 3 on saddle's opposite end.

Step 5: Stand horse upright. Pull, push, or twist legs until horse stands steadily on all four legs. Carefully lay horse on one end and drive a second nail halfway into upper cross-brace joint at either leg, near brace's top. Repeat on horse's other end after checking that horse still stands steady.

Step 6: Position 13½" lower cross brace so that its bottom just reaches from one leg's outside surface to the other's. Nail lower brace as you did the upper brace. Repeat on saddle's opposite end.

Step 7: Stand horse upright. Lay each 36" side brace on top of lower cross braces. Nail to legs, placing nails diagonally.

Step 8: Nail a 7½" end rail to saddle at each end of horse, aligning bottom of end rail flush with bottom of saddle.

Step 9: Place each side rail between end rails, laying it on top of upper cross braces. Nail through end rails into either end of each side rail to complete the trough.

Step 10: Drive all nails in. Bend ends of any nails protruding from legs' inner faces; hammer them flush with wood surface.

Step 11: Drape a piece of fabric evenly across trough. Secure with tacks placed at 3-inch intervals all along *outer* faces of side and end rails, leaving fabric slightly slack in trough.

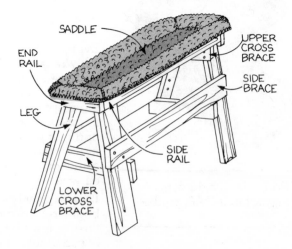

Putting the Cover On

Whether you come straight from stripping your furniture's old outer-cover fabric or from doctoring its insides, you should be ready to dress it in its new suit of clothes.

In the following pages, you'll learn how to insure the snug fit of your outer cover, using tacks or staples, and how to make the best use of cotton padding. Then you'll be led, step by step, through the re-covering of this book's featured fully upholstered armchair—you can apply most of what you learn about the armchair to your own furniture. You'll also be supplied with any re-covering technique variations necessary to adapt the basic how-to-do-it sections to the other furniture types in the Measurement Lists (pages 40–45). Then you'll be shown how to re-cover loose boxed cushions, and how to make a skirt and install it on your furniture. If you intend to use twine-held buttons, refer to page 95 for instructions.

Basic techniques

Dining chair, armchair, ottoman, wing sofa—no matter what you're re-covering, you'll need to follow certain basic techniques to insure a professional-looking job. They all require attention to details and, for the novice, plenty of time.

How to tack or staple

The general technique for securing outer-cover fabric is the same whether you use tacks or staples.

First, position an outer-cover section on the appropriate portion of the furniture, centering dominant motifs or matching stripes, if necessary. Make sure the fabric's weave parallels the lines of the furniture and that the proper allowances overhang the stuffing edges or frame. Anchor the top

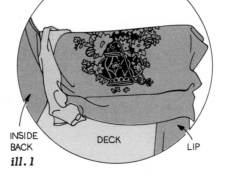

CENTER DOMINANT MOTIF ON INSIDE ARM, LETTING CORRECT ALLOWANCES OVERHANG ALL EDGES

INSIDE BACK   DECK   LIP

ill. 1

edge of the outer-cover section to the frame with slip tacks, placed every two to three inches. Then smooth the fabric of the section down, pull it taut, and slip-tack the section's bottom edge to the frame. (The term "slip-tacking" applies to staples as well as tacks. To keep staples from going all the way into the wood, hold the electric stapler ⅛ inch away from the surface.)

In general, you should tack from an edge's center toward its corners. A good way to keep the section's edges smooth is to grasp the fabric two to four inches away from the previous tack and pull it until it's taut. To keep the taut fabric from slipping while you get a tack on your tack hammer, press it against the furniture's frame,

halfway between your grip point and the previous tack, with your index and third fingers spread

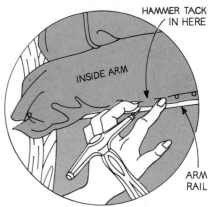

HAMMER TACK IN HERE

INSIDE ARM

ARM RAIL

PULL FABRIC TAUT; PRESS AGAINST FRAME TO PREVENT SLIPPAGE AS YOU PICK UP TACK ON TACK HAMMER

ill. 2

apart. Drive the tack into the frame between your two fingers. Repeat this technique for each succeeding tack.

Before slip-tacking the section's remaining edges, make any necessary cuts (see page 66). Snip each cut in stages as you push the deck, inside-arm, and inside-back outer covers through crevices to the furniture's outside. Then smooth and stretch the section's fabric with your hands. Finish slip-tacking and double-check the section's position before hammering the tacks all the way in.

If you used staples in slip-tacking, use pliers to remove a slip-tacked staple; then replace it with a new staple, driven all the way in. Continue to remove and replace the slip-tacked staples, one by one.

You'll finish securing the outer-cover section by driving in tacks or staples at 1 to 2-inch intervals around all edges.

Use #3 tacks or ⅜-inch staples to secure outer-cover fabric and most welt; #4 tacks or ⅜-inch staples to secure burlap, padding, and cardboard strips; and #2 tacks or ¼-inch staples to fasten fabric to the front arm panels and rim the panels with welt.

When the word "tack" appears in the rest of this chapter, substitute the word "staple" if that's what you intend to use.

Pleating

Pleating is used to hide excess fabric wherever a section must go around a curved area or corner. It is tricky and requires a special knack.

If you're pleating fabric to go around a curve, analyze the excess fullness of the outer-cover fabric requiring pleats; decide which direction you want the pleat folds to face, and estimate how many pleats you must make to crimp in all the excess fullness smoothly. Try out a pleat or two, holding them in position with your fingers, to see how they'll look and where they'll lie.

When you're ready to begin pleating, drive an initial holding tack all the way into the furniture's frame, through the outer-cover edge, just where you expect the inner fold of your first pleat to lie. This tack holds the rest of the outer-cover section smoothly in position and acts as a fulcrum against which to form the first pleat.

Form the first pleat so that its outer fold covers the holding

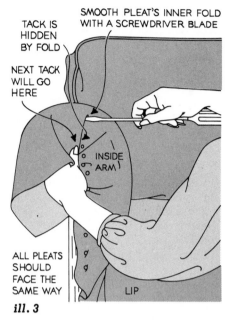

TACK IS HIDDEN BY FOLD

NEXT TACK WILL GO HERE

SMOOTH PLEAT'S INNER FOLD WITH A SCREWDRIVER BLADE

INSIDE ARM

ALL PLEATS SHOULD FACE THE SAME WAY

LIP

ill. 3

tack's head. Smooth the pleat's inner fold with a blunt edge such as a ruler or screwdriver blade.

The depth of each pleat will depend on the amount of fullness you're crimping in and the number of pleats you intend to make to achieve the desired smoothness. Keep the depth of each pleat and the distance between pleats uniform at top and bottom. As you form the pleats, remember that several small pleats look neater than one or two large ones.

If the fabric is heavy, making the pleats bulky, cut off each

PLEATING A CORNER ON A TIGHT SEAT

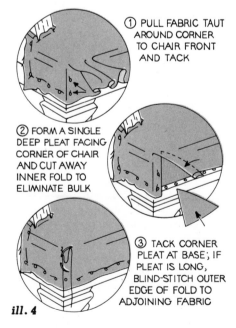

① PULL FABRIC TAUT AROUND CORNER TO CHAIR FRONT AND TACK

② FORM A SINGLE DEEP PLEAT FACING CORNER OF CHAIR AND CUT AWAY INNER FOLD TO ELIMINATE BULK

③ TACK CORNER PLEAT AT BASE; IF PLEAT IS LONG, BLIND-STITCH OUTER EDGE OF FOLD TO ADJOINING FABRIC

ill. 4

pleat's inner fold. To do so, begin on the first pleat, before the other pleats are formed. Cut into the pleat's bottom layer, ½ to 1 inch past the holding tack, while holding the outer fold out away from the furniture. The cut should end ¼ to 1 inch shy of the top of the outer fold. Next, cut into the pleat's middle layer ¼ to 1 inch shy of the outer fold. Make the second cut join the first cut, so as to remove a triangular piece of the middle and inner layers. Now press the pleat back into position against the furniture.

Drive a tack into the outer fold's edge, near the bottom edge of the pleat. Now move on to form the next pleat. Continue pleating until all the excess fullness has been taken in, and the outer-cover section rounds the curve neatly.

If you're pleating fabric to go around a corner, usually only one pleat is required to take in the excess fullness. Pull the fabric taut around the corner and tack it with one or two holding tacks, placed ½ to ¾ inch from the corner, to hold the fabric smoothly in place. Form the slack excess fabric into a pleat and cut off the pleat's inner fold, as directed above (see illustration 4). Then tack the outer fold's bottom edge down. If the pleat's outer fold is long, you may wish to blind-stitch it (see page 65) to the adjacent fabric that underlies the pleat, to keep the pleat flat.

Blind-tacking

Certain outside outer-cover sections—the front border or skirt, and the outside arms, back, and wings—must be blind-tacked so that the tacks (or staples) won't show. To handle a section that isn't trimmed with welt, fold the section's top edge seam allowance under (as in Step 3 on page 77) and slip-tack it to the furniture along the fold's edge. To handle welted sections, slip-tack the section's top edge to the furniture *immediately* beneath the welt cord. The slip tacks—placed at 4-inch intervals along the section's top edge—will hold the section in the correct position on the furniture as you blind-tack.

After slip-tacking the top edge, flip the section up, exposing the fabric's under-turned allowance. Tack the allowance to the underlying frame member. (The tacks should pass through the section's welt seam allowance, if there is one.)

Fold the section back down, right side out, and remove the slip tacks. Then flip it up again and lay a ½-inch-wide cardboard tacking strip on top of the allowance, aligning the strip's top edge with the allowance's folded edge. Slip-tack it into position, placing a slip tack at either end and one in the center of the strip.

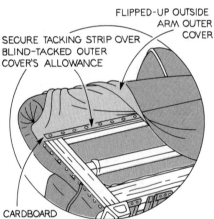

SECURE TACKING STRIP OVER BLIND-TACKED OUTER COVER'S ALLOWANCE

FLIPPED-UP OUTSIDE ARM OUTER COVER

CARDBOARD TACKING STRIP

ill. 5

Then tack the strip all along the section's allowance, driving the tacks through all underlying thicknesses into the frame member beneath. Finally, drive in the slip tacks. When you fold the section back down, right side out, the tacking strip underneath assures you of a tightly secured, straight top edge.

Over the cardboard strip under an outside-back or outside-arm section, you'll tack the top edges of the section's underlying burlap and padding. Over the strip under a front-border section, you'll tack the section's padding. A skirt needs nothing more under it than the cardboard strip.

Now bring the section back down, right side out. It will hide the tacks and tacking strip completely.

Preparing welt ends

Certain sections—an outside back, for instance—require tacked welt. To prepare a welt end for tacking, snip the tip of the end off (including the cord) at a 90° angle to the cord. Rip open an inch of the welt seam and snip off another ½ inch of cord. Open the loose flange flaps and fold the welt casing's end in over the cord end. Press the flange flaps together again. The last ½ inch of

PREPARING WELT ENDS

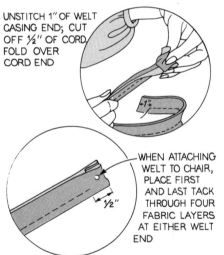

UNSTITCH 1" OF WELT CASING END; CUT OFF ½" OF CORD. FOLD OVER CORD END

WHEN ATTACHING WELT TO CHAIR, PLACE FIRST AND LAST TACK THROUGH FOUR FABRIC LAYERS AT EITHER WELT END

ill. 6

welt casing is now four fabric layers thick, rather than two. As you attach the welt to your furniture, you'll place your first tack into this last ½ inch. You'll also prepare the other end of the welt the same way, and place your final welt tack into the final ½ inch of welt casing.

Blind-stitching

Blind-stitching is used to sew outer-cover sections to each other in such a way that the stitches

don't show. It takes more time than blind-tacking, so you should use it only in places where blind-tacking is impossible.

You blind-stitch through both sides of the welt casing, just under the welt cord of a section if the welt has been tacked into position, as when joining the outside back to the outside arm and back boxing. You blind-stitch through one side of the welt casing, behind the welt cord, when attaching an unsecured section with welt machine-sewn to it to a secured section (as when sewing a skirt to the lip, outside arms, and outside back). Where no welt is present between two sections, you blind-stitch through the folded edge of the unsecured section's seam allowance, directly into the secured section.

To prepare for blind-stitching, align the unsecured outer-cover section over or abutting the secured outer-cover section to which it is to be sewn, and slip-tack or, with upholsterer's skewers, skewer it in place at 3-inch intervals, with its seam allowance folded under. The folded-under fabric will form its own pleats wherever you fit it to a curve. Cut a length of upholsterer's twine or heavy-duty polyester thread twice as long as the distance you wish to stitch. Knot one end of the twine with an overhand knot (see page 100). Thread a 3-inch curved needle.

Before you begin sewing two sections together, bury the knot inside the fold of the unsecured section's allowance, at one end of the opening to be sewn together, and take three hidden ¼-inch-long stitches, the first stitch running in the wrong direction, away from where you intend to blind-stitch, the second two stitches running back in the right direction, as shown in illustration 7, below.

Now begin blind-stitching. To make the stitches hidden, take a stitch in the secured outer-cover section, then move to the adjoining folded edge of the un-secured section, or the unsecured

HOW TO BLIND-STITCH

IF WELT IS TACKED IN PLACE, PASS NEEDLE UNDER WELT CORD IF WELT IS SEWN TO UN-SECURED SECTION, SEW THROUGH REAR OF WELT CASING

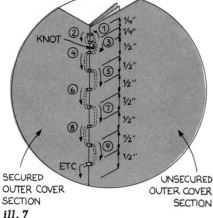

KNOT

¼"
¼"
½"
½"
½"
½"
½"
½"
½"

SECURED OUTER COVER SECTION

ETC.

UNSECURED OUTER COVER SECTION

ill. 7

section's welt, and set a stitch in it. (In certain situations, as when joining the outside back to the outside arm, you thrust the needle under the intervening tacked welt's cord to set the second stitch in the unsecured section's folded edge. Then thrust the needle back under the welt cord to set the third stitch in the secured section.) Continue to alternate stitches, back and forth between the two sections. The stitches should be strictly contiguous. When the needle emerges from one stitch, it should plunge directly into the adjoining section's fabric to make the next stitch, so that the twine is completely hidden from stitch to stitch. After every three stitches, gently pull the twine taut. Remove the slip tacks or skewers as you stitch.

To end your blind-stitching, blind-stitch backward for about two inches. Form an overhand

knot close to the fabric. Take a stitch, pushing the needle through the same hole from which it last emerged. Pull the twine taut with a jerk; the knot will pass back through the fabric. Snip the twine close to the fabric. Massage the fabric where you took the last stitch and the twine end will disappear.

Cuts to fit sections snugly

As you install the outer-cover sections on your furniture, you will need to make cuts in the edges of some sections in order to fit them around intervening frame members without bunching them up, pulling them into creases, or displaying their raw edges. Some cuts permit the fabric to straddle the arm and back posts smoothly. Others release fabric wedged between a post and an adjacent rail so that you can tack the fabric down evenly. Still others allow you to tuck the fabric under itself to edge an exposed leg top.

Cuts are made in an outer-cover section after you have aligned it on the appropriate portion of your furniture and have at least slip-tacked parts of the section's edges to hold it in position.

Many of the cuts must be made to fit a corner or edge of a section around a portion of the frame which is deep inside the furniture and not easily visible. In order to make such a cut accurate, you should fold the section corner or edge which is to be fitted around the hidden frame member back, wrong side up, over your hand. Then, pushing the fold forward with your fingertips, work the fold down into the hidden area of the furniture, just until you feel the edge of the frame member through the fabric with your fingertips. (If you can't reach the frame member with your fingertips, use a long screwdriver.) Marking with your finger or the screwdriver the spot where the section's fabric first encounters the frame member, pull the corner or edge back out. Your final cut should extend from the section's edge just as far as the spot

marked by your finger or the screwdriver.

No matter what kind of cut you're making, always make your initial cut a little shorter than you need to. Then push the fabric on either side of the cut around the frame member or between the frame and the stuffing and pull it taut. Gently tugging the fabric ends on either side of the cut, and then snipping the cut a little deeper, and tugging again and snipping again, deepen the cut just until the section's fabric lies smoothly around the frame member or members. If you sever too deeply into the section, you'll have an unsightly rent which, even if patched, will look unprofessional when the section is finally tacked or sewn into position.

Cotton padding

Without padding to fill out and soften its contours, your fabric-covered furniture would resemble a wrinkled man dressed as a youth.

Place a fresh layer of cotton under all fabric-covered surfaces. To increase your furniture's comfort, plan to leave the old padding in place on inside sections—the deck, inside arms, and back. Simply add a new layer of padding atop the old layers. However, if the old padding is in bad condition, replace it entirely with new padding of the same dimensions as the old padding, then add an extra new layer on top.

If the old padding on outside sections is in good condition, you can reuse it without any addition of new padding (the step-by-step instructions assume you must substitute new padding on outside sections).

Because you can buy cotton padding in 27-inch-wide rolls, you can ordinarily cover an entire section of your furniture with a single piece of new cotton padding.

To shape a layer of padding to fit a section of your furniture, begin by tearing off a piece of padding larger than the area of furniture to be covered. (Don't use shears to shape or sever cotton padding because cutting leaves a hard edge. Tear it with your fingers instead.) Lay the new padding over the old padding on the appropriate part of the furniture. Holding the padding in place with one hand, tear away the excess padding, one edge at a time, with the other hand until the new layer's edges conform to the old padding's shape. If you're replacing all the old padding, you may need to shape several layers of new padding until the desired thickness is achieved. (Remember the new padding will compact somewhat with age.)

High-backed love seats and sofas, and the inside backs of a variety of other furniture may be too large to cover with a single width of padding. In those cases, you must abut two or three pieces together to cover the surface. The loose fibers act as tiny hooks. You can form a continuous layer merely by pushing the padding pieces together and giving their jointures a few pats.

Use new padding also to fill in the gaps in old padding. Tear off a flat patch approximately the size of each gap (or a little larger) and lay it over the gap, patting it into place.

PLUMP OUT HOLLOW AREAS IN NEW COVER BY PUSHING IN LOOSE PADDING WITH A RULER OR SCREWDRIVER

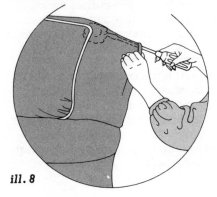

ill. 8

When installing pre-sewn parts of your new outer cover, use new padding in wads to plump out hollows under the cover.

Putting the cover on

While studying the following operations—basic to the recovering of most types of furniture—refer to the chair-frame illustration on page 96. It will help you identify the frame members of your furniture, and understand the cuts you must make to fit outer-cover fabric around them. Every frame member has four faces (unless it is perfectly round). If you examine your furniture's frame, you can identify its faces as follows: front faces are those facing forward; back faces are those facing backward; top faces are those facing upward; bottom faces are those facing downward; inner faces are those side faces which face toward the inside of the furniture; and outer faces are those side faces which face toward the outside of the furniture.

As you begin work, your furniture should be sitting upright on upholsterer's horses (unless otherwise designated). When you put it on the floor to work on the outside arms and back, make sure it sits on a rug, bedsheet, or tarpaulin to protect its cover and exposed wood from scratches and snags.

Step by step: Putting new outer cover and padding on a fully upholstered armchair's lip and deck

As you fit your lip/decking outer-cover section onto your chair, keep in mind that the lip's top front edge should be ½ inch higher than the decking behind it, to keep the deck cushion from slipping forward as you sit.

1 If you've not already done so, snip twine that moors the old lip/decking seam to underlying muslin or burlap. Pry out all re-

maining tacks holding old lip/decking outer-cover section to side and back rails. Peel off old lip/decking section. Leave old padding in place, if in good condition. Fill up any gaps in old deck and horizontal lip padding with new cotton. If old padding is disintegrating, substitute new padding (see page 66). Lip should be ½ inch higher than deck; build it up with a layer or more of new padding, if necessary.

2 Place lip portion of lip/decking outer-cover section over horizontal lip padding, positioning section's stitched corners exactly over underlying chair lip's corners. Fold one front corner of lip/decking section back, wrong side up. Start a cut in bottom edge of lip portion, one inch away from lip/decking seam, aiming the cut toward arm post (see illustration 9). Make the cut about four inches deep, paralleling the lip/decking seam. Grasp the lip's side fabric—the fabric to the rear of the cut—and push it under arm liner, behind arm post, to chair's outside (see illustration 10); pull it taut.

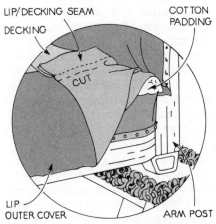

LIP/DECKING SEAM
DECKING
CUT
COTTON PADDING
LIP OUTER COVER
ARM POST

TO FIT LIP OUTER COVER AROUND ARM POST, CUT PARALLEL TO LIP/DECKING SEAM
ill. 9

You may need to deepen the cut a little more to make fabric at the side of the horizontal lip lie smooth. Working from chair's side, tug and snip only until all wrinkles disappear from lip's

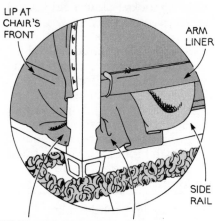

LIP AT CHAIR'S FRONT

ARM LINER

SIDE RAIL

WORK LIP OUTER COVER AROUND ARM POST TO CHAIR'S OUTSIDE

ill. 10

side. Slip-tack side fabric with one tack to side rail's top, next to arm post.

Repeat Step 2 to fit lip portion of outer cover around other arm post.

3 Fold decking back over lip and push lip and deck padding out of the way. Measure the distance across deck between inside arms, along line where lip meets deck (the lip/decking seam). Chalk a mark on the underlying burlap to designate the exact center of that distance. Pin the notch in lip/decking seam allowance to the center mark on burlap. Remove slip tacks placed to hold side fabric to side rails in Step 2. Pull lip/decking seam taut and retack side fabric to side rail's top on both sides, driving tacks all the way in.

Thread a 6-inch curved needle with a length of upholsterer's twine or heavy-duty polyester thread twice as long as lip/decking seam. At one end of seam, plunge needle through seam allowance into burlap, run needle under side edgewire, and pull it out through the vertically draped burlap at deck's side. Tie an upholsterer's slipknot at end of thread (see page 100); secure with an overhand knot (see page 100). Pull needle back over deck to prepare for sewing.

Moving one inch toward chair's center, plunge needle down through seam allowance, catch a spring's top coil or some spring twine in your stitch, and pull needle up again. Move another inch away for your next stitch. Continue stitching until you've crossed entire width of lip/decking seam.

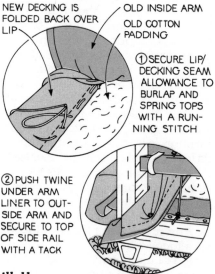

NEW DECKING IS FOLDED BACK OVER LIP

OLD INSIDE ARM

OLD COTTON PADDING

① SECURE LIP/ DECKING SEAM ALLOWANCE TO BURLAP AND SPRING TOPS WITH A RUNNING STITCH

② PUSH TWINE UNDER ARM LINER TO OUTSIDE ARM AND SECURE TO TOP OF SIDE RAIL WITH A TACK

ill. 11

In your last stitch, catch edgewire and push needle out through vertically draped burlap at deck's side. Then insinuate the needle through the crevice between deck and bottom of inside arm, bringing it through to chair's outside. Loop twine twice around needle before pulling twine taut. Tap a slip tack into side rail's top, wrap twine twice around tack's shank, and drive tack in. Cut off dangling end, leaving ½ inch of twine. Lay decking back over deck.

4 Lift vertical portion of lip/ decking outer-cover section gently; expose padding on lip. If necessary, remove old padding entirely and replace it with new padding (see page 66). Then shape a new layer of cotton padding to fit over chair's vertical lip area, from beneath edge roll down to front rail's top. (Padding should not extend over front rail.) Press it into position on lip.

Shape another layer of padding (see page 66) long enough to

extend over the first—from lip/ decking seam, over edge roll, to front rail's top—and wide enough to extend from inside arm to inside arm. Press it into position on lip.

If you plan to add a skirt, lip's outer cover will extend to chair's bottom, but padding still will extend only to front rail's top (same height as skirt's top edge).

5 Gently pull vertical portion of lip/decking outer-cover section back down over new padding.

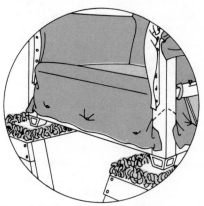

PULL LIP OUTER COVER TAUT AND SECURE AT THREE POINTS ALONG MIDDLE OF FRONT RAIL'S FRONT

ill. 12

At one corner, pull lip's outer-cover section taut toward chair's bottom in a straight line down from the corner. Slip-tack section to front rail's front with one tack, about one inch below front rail's top and two inches shy of arm post. Pull and tack section at lip's other corner in the same way, and then do it midway between these two corner tacks. (Don't worry if section is still slightly wrinkled at corners next to arm posts.)

6 At each corner and at the midway point, check lip's front-edge height, measuring from lip's front edge to front rail's bottom. The distance should be the same at all three points, making the lip level so it eventually

can support the deck cushion evenly. If lip's edge isn't level, retack outer cover as in Step 5.

If lip's front edge is level, drive slip tacks in; tack bottom edge of lip's outer-cover section at 2-inch intervals all across front of front rail. Place the tacks at least one inch below front rail's top; later you will tack skirt's or front border's top edge between lip's bottom edge and rail's top.

Vertical lip outer-cover fabric will pucker slightly at corners next to arm posts. Don't worry about that for now.

7 Fold decking back over lip. Shape a new layer of cotton padding to fit deck (replace old padding too, if necessary—see page 66). Make sure old and new deck paddings' front edges lie snug against lip/decking seam. Fold decking back to cover deck padding; smooth it toward inside back. Push decking's side edges through crevice between deck and inside arm to chair's outside.

8 Fold left rear corner of decking section back over itself, wrong side up. Run your hand under the flap of fabric and push the fold back under inside back toward back post, pushing until you can feel the post under the fabric with your fingertips. Then begin a cut: starting about one inch to the right of the corner of the flap lying over your hand, cut from the corner's edge in toward the post, using your hand's edge as guide. Cut as far as you can.

Push decking on either side of cut around back post to chair's outside. Standing at chair's rear corner, and poking shears around post, tug gently on decking and snip cut deeper until decking section lies smooth over that corner of the deck.

Repeat Step 8 to fit decking around other back post, starting cut one inch to the left of the right rear corner flap.

9 Stand at chair's rear. Decking's rear edge should protrude from beneath back liner. Fold triangular flap of excess over the decking so fold abuts the back post; trim flap off to within 1½ inches of fold. Fold remaining 1½-inch flap under at left-hand side of decking's rear edge. Pull decking's rear edge taut at left-hand side. Slip-tack folded portion of decking to back rail's top with one tack, an inch shy of back post. Fold, trim, pull, and slip-tack triangular excess flap at right-hand side of decking's rear edge in the same way. Then pull and slip-tack decking's rear edge at the midway point between the first two corner tacks.

Stand at chair's side. Decking's side edge should protrude from beneath arm liner. Fold, trim, pull, and slip-tack triangular flap of excess at rear of decking's side edge to side rail's top as you did decking's rear edge to back

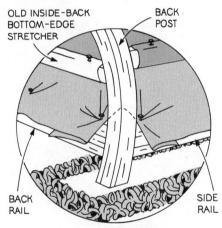

OLD INSIDE-BACK BOTTOM-EDGE STRETCHER

BACK POST

BACK RAIL

SIDE RAIL

CUT DECKING TO FIT AROUND BACK POST. FOLD CUT'S RAW EDGES UNDER AND TACK TO SIDE AND BACK RAIL TOPS
ill. 13

rail's top. Pull and slip-tack decking's side edge with one more tack, placed on side rail's top, midway between lip/decking seam and back post. Repeat slip-tacking process on chair's other side.

When slip-tacking, pull decking taut enough to remove wrinkles but not so taut as to depress deck.

10 Above where front rail's top meets arm post, you'll note

that lip's outer-cover fabric is still slightly puckered. To release those folds, start a cut into bunched fabric between lip and arm post, while gently tugging fabric in front of and below cut just until puckers disappear and vertical portion of lip drapes smoothly when pulled down at corner.

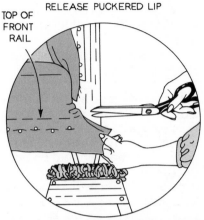

TOP OF FRONT RAIL

RELEASE PUCKERED LIP

AT CORNER OF LIP, SNIP CAREFULLY UPWARD INTO FABRIC BUNCHED AT ARM POST, TUGGING AS YOU GO, UNTIL FABRIC PULLS SMOOTH. DON'T CUT TOO FAR
ill. 14

Fill any hollows under outer cover in vertical lip area near arm post with wads of padding, packed in place as smoothly as possible with a screwdriver.

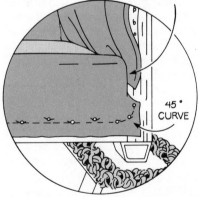

FILL HOLLOWS IN VERTICAL LIP NEAR ARM POST WITH WADS OF PADDING

45° CURVE

TACK LOOSE FRONT FLAP OF LIP OUTER COVER TO FRONT OF ARM POST AT A 45° ANGLE TO LAST TACK ALONG FRONT RAIL
ill. 15

Folding its raw edge under, tack remaining loose front flap of outer-cover fabric (created by cut) to arm post's front, arching a curved line of tacks, spaced at 2-inch intervals, up at a 45° angle from tacks on front rail's front. Push the small flap of fabric—to the rear of the cut—behind arm post to chair's outside; pull it taut and tack it with one tack to side rail's top, over lip section's side fabric tacked to side rail in Steps 2 and 3.

Repeat Step 10 on lip's outer cover at other arm post.

11 Secure decking's side and rear edges to side and back rails' tops with slip tacks placed at 2-inch intervals. Double-check your work; there should be no gap between deck and inside arm. If there *is* a gap, remove slip tacks and shove wads of loose padding up under decking to fill gap as smoothly as possible; re-tack. When gap is closed, drive slip tacks in.

Step by step: Putting new outer cover and padding on a fully upholstered armchair's inside arms

In order to insure that both inside arms are symmetrical in their padding, pleating, and finishing, we suggest you work on both arms simultaneously. Apply each step first to one inside arm, then the other, before continuing to the next step.

1 Pry out any tacks holding old inside-arm outer-cover section to frame. Peel off old inside-arm section. Leave old padding in place, filling up any gaps with new padding (or replace old padding entirely, if necessary—see page 66). Shape a layer of new padding to blanket the old one. The new padding layer should extend about ½ inch beyond all edges. Tuck the edges of

the new padding into all crevices.

Lay new inside-arm outer-cover section over padding, centering dominant motifs or stripes (if any) and making sure the correct allowances overhang all edges.

2 Slip-tack inside-arm outer-cover section's front top edge to arm post's outer face with one tack, placed at inside arm/outside arm junction (see illustration 16). Then smooth section down along inside arm's front edge and tack section's front edge to arm post's front with one tack at lip height.

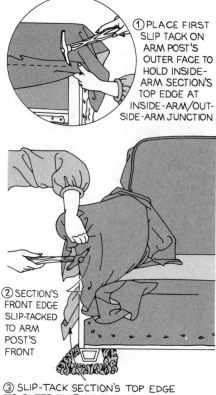

① PLACE FIRST SLIP TACK ON ARM POST'S OUTER FACE TO HOLD INSIDE-ARM SECTION'S TOP EDGE AT INSIDE-ARM/OUTSIDE-ARM JUNCTION

② SECTION'S FRONT EDGE SLIP-TACKED TO ARM POST'S FRONT

③ SLIP-TACK SECTION'S TOP EDGE TO OUTER FACE OF ARM RAIL

④ CUT INTO SECTION'S BOTTOM EDGE

ill. 16

Finally, slip-tack section's front edge to arm post's front with another tack in a vertical line directly above previous tack and level with first tack.

3 Working from inside arm's front edge toward its rear, and keeping the weave of the inside-arm outer-cover section aligned straight along arm of chair from back to front and top to bottom; slip-tack section's top

edge to outer face of arm rail (along inside arm/outside arm junction). Place tacks at 2-inch intervals, working toward chair's rear and tacking just until you are below front edge of back boxing (do not tack all the way to chair's rear).

4 Smooth inside-arm outer-cover section down; let section's bottom edge overlap deck, pushed slightly into crevice between deck and inside arm. Without folding lower front corner of section back, make the same kind of cut you made in lip/decking outer-cover section (Step 2, page 67). Start cut where edge of inside-arm section lies over lip/decking seam and aim toward arm post. Cut should be about four inches deep. Push the section's bottom edge—the portion to the rear of the cut—down through inside arm/deck crevice.

Pull bottom edge of the section—the portion to the front of the cut—around arm post's front; slip-tack it to post's front with one tack at the level of arm liner's bottom.

5 At crevice between inside arm and inside back, fold inside-arm outer-cover section's whole rear edge back, wrong side up. Run your hand under the flap of fabric and slide fold one inch into crevice. At the level of arm liner's bottom (about one inch above the deck), start a cut into inside-arm outer-cover section's rear edge, parallel to deck. This cut will eventually have a "Y" shape, to fit section around back liner. Cut the stem of the "Y" to within six inches of inside arm/inside back crevice. Then cut the "Y's" arms, each one inch long, so their ends span the back liner's thickness.

As best you can, push lower portion of inside-arm outer-cover section's rear edge—that portion below the cut—under back liner to chair's outside back. Push the rest of section's bottom edge—the part still resting on deck—through deck/inside arm crevice and under arm liner to chair's outside arm.

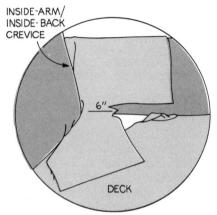

INSIDE-ARM/
INSIDE-BACK
CREVICE

6"

DECK

FOLD INSIDE-ARM SECTION'S REAR EDGE BACK AND CUT TO WITHIN 6" OF INSIDE-ARM/ INSIDE-BACK CREVICE, ALONG ARM LINER'S BOTTOM

ill. 17

6 Stand at chair's side. You'll see the inside-arm outer-cover section's bottom edge bunched around back post. Start a cut into section's bottom edge where side rail's top meets back post's front. Cut upward as far as arm liner's bottom, toward arm liner/back post junction. Pull split section taut around back post, snipping cut a little deeper, if necessary, to pull lower rear inside-arm outer cover smooth.

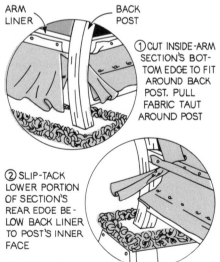

ARM LINER

BACK POST

① CUT INSIDE-ARM SECTION'S BOTTOM EDGE TO FIT AROUND BACK POST. PULL FABRIC TAUT AROUND POST

② SLIP-TACK LOWER PORTION OF SECTION'S REAR EDGE BELOW BACK LINER TO POST'S INNER FACE

ill. 18

Standing at chair's rear, you should see lower portion of inside-arm outer-cover section's rear edge protruding from beneath back liner, near back post. Pull it taut and slip-tack it, bunched between back liner and back rail, to post's inner face, using three tacks placed at ½-inch intervals.

7 Upper portion of inside-arm outer-cover section's rear edge should be folded back over top of inside arm and one inch of fold should have been slid into inside arm/inside back crevice in Step 5. Push a screwdriver or ruler, laid on top of turned-back inside-arm section, through inside arm/inside back crevice at arm's top, to touch back post. Start a cut into inside-arm section's rear edge, two inches away, on deck side of tool. Cut toward back post, parallel to tool; end cut two inches short of inside back.

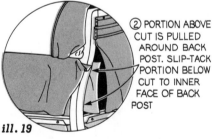

BACK POST

CUT

① LOCATE INNER FACE OF BACK POST WITH SCREWDRIVER. USE TOOL AS GUIDE IN MAKING CUT INTO INSIDE-ARM SECTION'S UPPER REAR EDGE TO WITHIN 2" OF INSIDE ARM/INSIDE BACK CREVICE

② PORTION ABOVE CUT IS PULLED AROUND BACK POST. SLIP-TACK PORTION BELOW CUT TO INNER FACE OF BACK POST

ill. 19

With screwdriver, push the portion of inside-arm outer-cover section's rear edge below most recent cut through inside arm/ inside back crevice to chair's outside, above back liner and alongside back post. Pull the portion of inside-arm section's rear edge above most recent cut around back post's outer face.

Stand at chair's rear. You should see the portion of inside-

arm outer-cover section below most recent cut protruding above back liner. Pull it taut and slip-tack its bottom edge to back post's inner face, just above back liner, using two tacks placed ½ inch apart. Smooth section upward and slip-tack its top edge to back post's inner face, using two more tacks, ½ inch apart.

Stand at chair's side. Grasp portion of inside-arm outer-cover section above most recent cut and pull it taut around back post's outer face. Slip-tack it to back post's back, using two tacks, placed an inch apart.

8 Starting at the front and working along chair's outside toward its rear, slip-tack inside-arm outer-cover section's bottom edge to side rail's top. Place slip tacks at 2-inch intervals; keep the weave of the fabric running straight up and down.

9 Finish slip-tacking inside-arm outer-cover section's top edge to outer face of arm rail (along inside arm/outside arm junction), placing tacks at 2-inch intervals and working from just below front edge of back boxing to rear edge of back post's outer face. As you near the arm's rear, pull section's top rear corner down and toward outside back to achieve smoothness over arm top before placing the last few slip tacks along arm rail. You may need to form one or two pleats (see page 64) in section's top edge, where it meets arm rail, to take up excess fabric and make the section lie smoothly over arm top's curve, above arm rail. Most of these pleats will eventually be hidden by the outside-arm outer-cover section.

Scrutinize your work: if pleats are regular and inside-arm outer-cover section fits smoothly along arm top, drive slip tacks all the way in along arm rail.

10 Where arm top meets back post's front, you'll notice that a flap of inside-arm outer-cover section's fabric still remains bunched up where section rounds the back post. Remove slip tacks placed to hold fabric to back post's back in Step 7. Start a cut into the flap, cutting downward, ½ inch in front of back post, into bunched fabric. Snip while gently

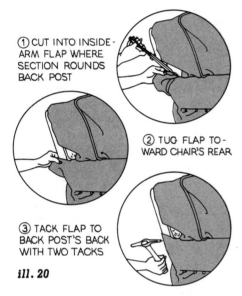

① CUT INTO INSIDE-ARM FLAP WHERE SECTION ROUNDS BACK POST

② TUG FLAP TOWARD CHAIR'S REAR

③ TACK FLAP TO BACK POST'S BACK WITH TWO TACKS

ill. 20

tugging flap toward chair's rear, just until fabric pulls smoothly around back post's outer face. Fold raw top edge of flap under, pull flap taut around back post, smooth it upward, and tack it to back post's back with two tacks, one tack ½ inch above the other.

11 Stand at chair's front. Starting at the level of arm liner's top, tack inside-arm outer-cover section's front edge to arm post's front at 1-inch intervals, smoothing the fabric upward and around from inside arm to arm front as you work. Place tacks along arm post front's center; stop tacking where post begins its outward curve.

12 You'll notice that inside-arm outer-cover section's front edge has considerable excess fullness where arm post curves outward, above last tack in previous step. Take in this fullness by forming pleats as explained on page 64 and in illustration 4, starting at the point at which you stopped tacking in Step 11, and continuing as far as inside arm/outside arm junction, until all fullness is crimped in and fabric lies neatly. Pleats should radiate outward like spokes toward arm top's curve; the last pleat should be formed at the level of inside arm/outside arm junction. Fabric's edge will still protrude from center of pleated area; this excess will be trimmed off later.

To make sure you end up with the same number of pleats on both arms, complete pleats on first arm; then measure distance between each pleat's inner and outer fold. Duplicate each pleat's dimensions on the second arm.

13 Aiming toward first slip tack placed in arm post in Step 2, start a cut into inside-arm outer-cover section's top edge, where section's top front corner is bunched beneath pleated area on arm's front.

CUT INTO INSIDE-ARM SECTION UNTIL SHEARS TOUCH INSIDE-ARM/OUTSIDE-ARM JUNCTION

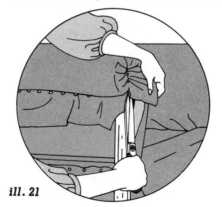

ill. 21

Roughly paralleling arm post's front, snip upward until shears touch inside arm/outside arm junction and section's bunched corner is released. Pull portion of section under pleats—the portion

to the arm-front side of cut—taut and tack it to arm post's front with one tack. If original slip tack (placed in Step 2) is causing fabric to wrinkle, remove it and retack.

14 In Step 4, you made a cut in inside-arm outer-cover section's lower front corner, and pulled the foremost portion of section's bottom edge around front of arm post, tacking it at arm post's front. Now, starting where front rail's top meets arm post, you must begin a cut into this foremost portion of section, in order to smooth inside-arm outer-cover section down the arm post alongside the vertical lip. Snip upward into foremost portion of section, paralleling vertical edge of lip and gently tugging section's front corner below the cut until foremost portion of inside-arm section pulls smoothly down along front of arm post, without bunching in crevice between lip and inside arm.

Fold raw inner edge of foremost portion—the edge of the cut you just made—under so that when foremost portion is pulled down along arm post, fold is parallel to vertical lip/inside arm crevice.

Pull foremost portion of inside-arm section down tautly along arm post's front. Near bottom edge of foremost portion, drive a tack through folded *inner* edge into arm post's front just above leg. Drive two more tacks in above the first, each an inch above the last. Now foremost portion of inside-arm outer-cover section is ready for stuffing.

Using a screwdriver or upholsterer's skewer, prod wads of padding into foremost portion of inside-arm outer-cover section tacked to lower arm post's front until the fold abutting the vertical lip is rounded out.

① CUT INTO FORE-MOST PORTION OF INSIDE ARM IN ORDER TO SMOOTH SECTION DOWN ARM POST

② PROD WADS OF PADDING INTO FOREMOST PORTIONS. FOLD ALONGSIDE LIP

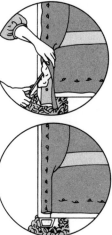

ill. 22

③ CLOSE FOLD WITH TACKS PLACED AT 1" INTERVALS

Secure padding in fold by tacking opposite edge of inside-arm outer-cover section's foremost portion to arm post's front at opposite side of padding from the fold. Tack vertically, placing tacks at 1-inch intervals, from leg's top up to the level of arm liner's bottom.

15 Double-check your work on inside-arm outer-cover section up to this point. If satisfied that all is ship-shape, drive in the slip tacks securing section's bottom edge to side rail's top. Stop within four inches of back post.

16 Stand at chair's rear. Remove slip tacks you used in Step 7 to secure a portion of inside-arm outer-cover section's rear edge to back post's inner face, above back liner. Tug on this portion of section until inside-arm outer cover is taut across visible surface of inside arm. Holding it taut, retack section's rear edge to back post's inner face, above back liner, driving tacks all the way in.

Drive in slip tacks holding a lower portion of inside-arm

outer-cover section's rear edge to inner face of back post *below* back liner.

Step by step: Putting new front border and padding on a fully upholstered armchair's front

Though these step-by-step instructions assume you have planned to have a front border, you may have planned to eliminate the front border and add a skirt in its place. For more information on skirts, see pages 92–95. If you're planning a skirt, skip this phase of outer-cover installation and go on to your inside back (page 74). Add the skirt at the very end.

1 To prepare for installation of front-border outer-cover section, trim off all excess fabric from lip outer-cover section at lip's bottom edge to within ½ inch of tacks across lip's bottom. Also cut off any inside-arm outer-cover section fabric dangling down over leg tops.

Trim off any excess fabric from pleats at arm posts' tops and from inside-arm outer-cover sections' front edges, to within ½ inch of tacks on arm posts' fronts.

Place chair on its back on floor.

2 Slip a thin ruler between tacks securing lip outer-cover section's bottom edge, to push up any cotton padding that may have been pulled down below front rail's top as you tacked lip outer-cover section in place.

3 Position front-border outer-cover section against chair front so front border and lip motifs match and front-border section's top-edge welt runs along front rail's top. Place a slip tack at center of section's top, just beneath welt cord. Pulling welt taut, slip-tack section's top edge at each arm post's front, just beneath welt cord.

POSITION FRONT BORDER SO THAT ITS MOTIF MATCHES LIP MOTIF. SLIP-TACK ITS TOP EDGE AT CENTER AND AT EACH END

ill. 23

Check to be sure front-border section's height is even all across chair front by measuring from welt to front rail's bottom in several places. Reposition section and slip-tack again if section is not evenly aligned. Add slip tacks at 4-inch intervals between first three tacks.

4 Lift front-border outer-cover section and lay it back over lip; blind-tack its top-edge allowance at 4-inch intervals to front rail's front, as directed on page 64. After removing slip tacks installed in Step 3, cut a cardboard tacking strip as long as chair is wide. Tack it into position over section's allowance, placing tacks at 2-inch intervals.

5 Shape a new layer of padding (see page 66) so padding extends from chair's bottom to twice front border's height (you'll double the padding over). Padding's width should reach arm

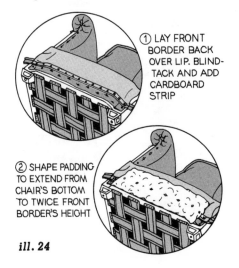

① LAY FRONT BORDER BACK OVER LIP. BLIND-TACK AND ADD CARDBOARD STRIP

② SHAPE PADDING TO EXTEND FROM CHAIR'S BOTTOM TO TWICE FRONT BORDER'S HEIGHT

ill. 24

posts at either side, but not extend over arm posts at all. Tack padding to front rail's front over cardboard tacking strip, with tacks placed at 4-inch intervals. Fold upper half of padding down over tacks (padding's upper layer will hide hollows formed by tacks).

6 Pull front-border outer-cover section down over padding, making sure padding's folded edge sits directly under front-border section's welt. Pulling section taut, slip-tack its bottom edge to front rail's bottom, next to each leg. Then slip-tack it midway between first two tacks. Working from center tack toward sides, slip-tack section's bottom edge all the way across front rail's bottom at 2-inch intervals. Drive slip tacks in.

7 From left front leg's center, start diagonal cut into front-border outer-cover section's lower left edge, near section's corner. End the cut where front rail's bottom meets left leg's inner edge.

Trim off section's lower left corner horizontally along front of leg, one inch below leg's top. Fold that remaining inch under so that fold's edge is just at leg's top. Tack fold horizontally just above leg's top with 2 tacks, placed at 1-inch intervals.

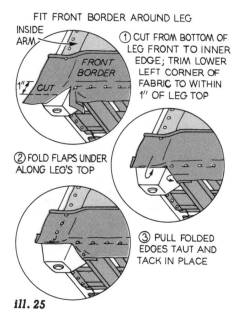

FIT FRONT BORDER AROUND LEG

INSIDE ARM

FRONT BORDER

1" CUT

① CUT FROM BOTTOM OF LEG FRONT TO INNER EDGE; TRIM LOWER LEFT CORNER OF FABRIC TO WITHIN 1" OF LEG TOP

② FOLD FLAPS UNDER ALONG LEG'S TOP

③ PULL FOLDED EDGES TAUT AND TACK IN PLACE

ill. 25

Tack length of front-border section to arm post's front in a direct line down from tacks on inside-arm outer-cover section's front edge at arm post's front. Place tacks at 1-inch intervals, tacking until you reach fold at leg's top. Trim off outside left edge of front-border section to within ½ inch of tacks.

Fold under the flap of front-border section abutting left leg's inner face. Tack fold to bottom of front rail, next to leg, using one tack.

Repeat Step 7 on front-border section at right front leg.

Step by step: Putting new outer cover and padding on a fully upholstered armchair's inside back

If you're a beginner, you may find the inside back/back boxing outer-cover section your last major hurdle in the reupholstering of your chair. You'll minimize your frustrations by working slowly, and by paying careful attention to the instructions and illustrations that follow.

1 Return chair to an upright position on upholsterer's horses.

2 Pry out any tacks holding old inside back/back boxing outer-cover section to frame. Peel off old inside back/back boxing section. Leaving old padding in place (unless it must be replaced—see page 66), fill up any gaps with new padding. Shape a layer of new padding to blanket the old padding on both inside-back and back-boxing portions of the furniture. Tuck new layer's edges into all crevices. If new padding is not wide enough to extend across entire inside back to reach outside back on both sides, piece several large pieces of padding together (see page 66).

3 Fold back-boxing portion of the outer-cover section back over inside-back portion, wrong side out. Position inside-back por-

tion of section, right side out, over inside back's padding, aligning it so notch in inside-back section's top-edge seam allowance sits exactly in center of back's top front edge.

Hold inside back's padding in place at one upper corner with one hand as you pull top of visible back boxing portion right side out over the corner with other hand. Once you've tugged visible back boxing into position, slip-tack its top rear edge to top of back post's back with one tack.

SLIP-TACK TOP REAR EDGE OF VISIBLE BACK BOXING TO TOP OF BACK POST'S BACK WITH ONE TACK

NEW PADDING

ill. 26

Repeat with remaining visible back boxing on opposite upper corner of back. Then place a third slip tack between the first two, attaching center of visible back boxing's top rear edge to top rail's top.

4 Lower sides of back-boxing portion of outer-cover section are still inside out, resting on arm tops. Pull up one side of lower back boxing from arm; start a cut into outer edge of stretcher attached to hidden-back-boxing portion of outer-cover section, one inch below the visible back boxing/hidden back boxing seam (see illustration 27). Cut six inches in toward inside back/back boxing seam, parallel to visible back boxing/hidden back boxing seam.

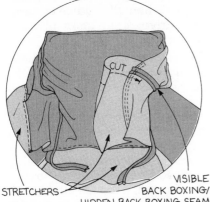

1" BELOW VISIBLE BACK BOXING/HIDDEN BACK BOXING SEAM, CUT AT LEAST 6" TOWARD INSIDE BACK/HIDDEN BACK BOXING SEAM

STRETCHERS

VISIBLE BACK BOXING/HIDDEN BACK BOXING SEAM

CUT

ill. 27

Tuck visible-back-boxing portion of outer-cover section—the portion above the cut—into crevice between inside back and arm top; pull section's rear edge alongside back post's outer face and slip-tack it loosely with one tack to back post's back. With the help of a long screwdriver, push upper portion of hidden back boxing and its stretcher—the portion below the cut—through the inside arm/inside back crevice to chair's outside back, passing the fabric above back liner and to inside of back post's inner face. Pull rear top corner of stretcher around and slip-tack it to back post's back, one inch above arm top level, with one tack.

Repeat Step 4 on opposite lower side of back-boxing portion of outer-cover section.

5 On one side of inside-back portion of outer-cover section, make a 3-inch-deep cut, paralleling welt end which dangles from inside back/back boxing outer-cover section's bottom edge. Cut should start at side edge of inside-back portion's bottom-edge stretcher, about 1½ inches below inside back/stretcher seam. Then cut should go upward through upper corner of stretcher, roughly parallel to welt (about one inch inside the inside back/welt seam), and continue on 1½ inches up into

inside-back portion of outer-cover section. This cut enables inside-back portion and welt to split around back post.

Repeat same cut on opposite side of inside-back portion of outer-cover section.

Starting at outer edge of a hidden-back-boxing portion's stretcher, two inches above stretcher's bottom edge, make an 8-inch-deep cut across stretcher and hidden-back-boxing portion of outer-cover section, aiming shears slightly upward so that you end cut three inches above stretcher/boxing's bottom edge. This cut allows hidden-back-boxing portion to straddle the back liner.

Repeat same cut on opposite hidden-back-boxing portion and its stretcher.

Push each welt end dangling from inside back/back boxing section's bottom edge through inside arm/deck crevice and out at chair's outside arm. Push inside-back portion's bottom-edge stretcher through inside back/deck crevice to chair's outside back. Push hidden-back-boxing portion and its stretcher—the portion above the most recent cut—through inside arm/inside back crevice to outside back, above back liner and inside back post's inner face.

CUTS NEEDED TO FIT INSIDE-BACK OUTER COVER AROUND FRAME

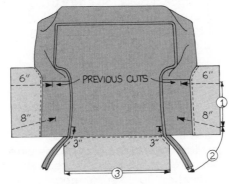

6"   PREVIOUS CUTS   6"
8"   8" ①
       3"   3"
          ③   ②

① PUSH ABOVE BACK LINER
② PUSH BETWEEN ARM LINER AND SIDE RAIL
③ PUSH THROUGH INSIDE BACK/DECK CREVICE
ill. 28

Push hidden-back-boxing portion and its stretcher—the portion below the most recent cut—

through inside arm/deck crevice and out at chair's outside arm (where you pushed welt end through).

Do the same for hidden-back-boxing portion and its stretcher at opposite side of inside back.

Stand at chair's rear. At either side of chair's back, slip-tack upper rear edge of hidden-back-boxing stretchers to back posts' backs, above back liner, tacking at 2-inch intervals.

Stand at chair's side. Tug at welt end until welt is snug against inside arm/inside back crevice. Slip-tack welt end to side rail's top with one tack, three inches from back post. Repeat with welt end at chair's other side.

6 If inside back/back boxing outer-cover section's top corners jut out and aren't stuffed enough, square them off by stuffing them with wads of padding, thrust in with a long screwdriver (see illustration 8 on page 67).

7 At 1-inch intervals, starting an inch below the slip tack placed in Step 3 at top of back post's back, tack visible-back-boxing portion's rear edge to back post's back, working vertically down post to within three inches of arm top.

You'll note that visible back boxing bunches slightly over arm top's curve, as it emerges from crevice at arm top. Start a cut into

START A CUT INTO BACK BOXING'S REAR EDGE WHERE IT BUNCHES AT ARM TOP
ill. 29

back boxing's rear edge, just where it bunches at arm top. Tugging visible back boxing above cut, snip cut until the back boxing can be pulled smoothly around back post's back. Tuck the portion of back boxing below cut back down into crevice at arm top. Fold under raw bottom edge of the portion of visible back boxing above cut and pull its rear edge to back post's back, tugging it down tautly as you slip-tack it to back post's back with one tack.

Stand at chair's side. Tug downward on the portion of hidden-back-boxing stretcher you pushed through to outside arm in Step 5. This tugging should pull lower front portion of visible back boxing snug against arm top. Tack hidden-back-boxing stretcher to side rail's top with two tacks.

If there are still hollows in visible back boxing's padding above arm top, fill them up with wads of padding, pushed up between arm top and back boxing with the help of a screwdriver.

Complete tacking of visible back boxing's rear edge to back post's back, tacking all the way down to arm top. Drive remaining slip tacks all the way into back post's back.

Repeat Step 7 on visible back boxing at opposite side of chair.

8 Working from center slip tack at top rail's back, smooth visible-back-boxing outer-cover section's top rear edge over rail and slip-tack it to top rail's back, working first to left corner and then to right corner. Place slip tacks an inch apart, tacking to within one inch of left and right back posts. Just shy of each post, form a pleat (see page 64) to take up excess fullness at top rear corners of visible back boxing. Pleats' outer folds should face each other. Tack pleats down and drive in all slip tacks at top rail's back.

9 Still standing at chair's rear, pull inside-back outer-cover section's bottom-edge stretcher taut and slip-tack it to center of back rail's top with one tack. Then work toward the left, slip-tacking stretcher's bottom edge to back rail's top at 2-inch intervals until you reach stretcher's left side edge. Do the same, working to stretcher's right side edge.

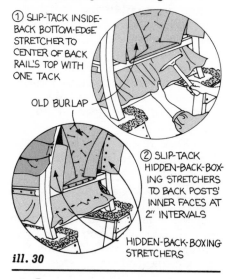

① SLIP-TACK INSIDE-BACK BOTTOM-EDGE STRETCHER TO CENTER OF BACK RAIL'S TOP WITH ONE TACK

OLD BURLAP

② SLIP-TACK HIDDEN-BACK-BOX-ING STRETCHERS TO BACK POSTS' INNER FACES AT 2" INTERVALS

HIDDEN-BACK-BOXING STRETCHERS

ill. 30

10 Remove slip tacks holding hidden-back-boxing outer-cover section's stretchers to back posts' backs above back liner. Pull stretchers taut. Slip-tack one stretcher's rear edge to back post's inner face with one tack placed just above back liner at stretcher's bottom edge. Then smooth stretcher upward and slip-tack it at its top edge to back post's inner face. Slip-tack it at 2-inch intervals in between top and bottom tacks. Repeat on stretcher at other side, slip-tacking it to opposite back post's inner face.

Check that the inside-back outer-cover section's visible surface is smooth and even across inside back of the chair. One side should not bulge out more than the other. To be sure, measure along inside arms from inside back to lip/decking seam. Distance must be the same on both sides or you'll have trouble fitting your deck cushion snugly against the inside back (see page 87). If inside back is bulging unevenly, remove slip tacks from hidden-

back-boxing stretchers again; repull them to adjust bulges and retack them to back posts' inner faces. When all is adjusted properly, drive all slip tacks all the way in.

Shape deck-cushion faces now. Though you will sew your deck cushion's outer cover later, this is the point at which you should give final shape to your deck-cushion faces (see page 87 for instructions). In so doing, you may discover that your cushions' chalked side outlines are so dissimilar that, once the cushion is assembled, you won't be able to turn it over when one face wears or is soiled. A lack of symmetry in your deck-cushion faces is caused by a lack of symmetry in your chair's inside arms and back. Before going any further in putting your new outer cover on, you should adjust these portions of your outer cover to achieve symmetry. The best way to do so is to remove the narrower arm's outer cover and add more padding. Then replace the inside arm's outer cover (see pages 70–73), adjust the inside-back outer cover (Step 10 on this page), and try outlining your cushion faces again. If there are still discrepancies, keep adjusting the inside-arm and inside-back outer covers until all is symmetrical.

Step by step: Putting new outer cover, burlap, and padding on a fully upholstered armchair's outside arms

You can begin and finish attaching one outside-arm outer-cover section before starting to work on the other because, unlike the inside arms, outside arms need not be perfectly symmetrical.

1 Now that you've secured the inside-back outer-cover section's welt end and the lower portion of hidden-back-boxing stretcher to side rail (in Steps 5 and 7 on page 75), finish tacking inside-arm outer-cover section's bottom edge to side rail's top. Tack it all the way to back post. Trim inside-arm section's bottom and top edges to within ½ inch of tacks.

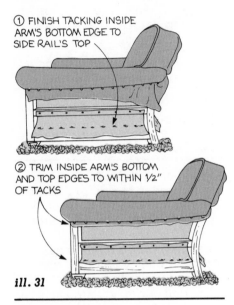

① FINISH TACKING INSIDE ARM'S BOTTOM EDGE TO SIDE RAIL'S TOP

② TRIM INSIDE ARM'S BOTTOM AND TOP EDGES TO WITHIN ½" OF TACKS

ill. 31

2 Set chair on its left side on floor.

3 Place outside-arm outer-cover section in position on outside arm of chair, so allowances extend evenly over its front, rear, top, and bottom edges. Check to make sure any dominant motifs are centered correctly, and that fabric's weave is straight. Slip-tack outside-arm section's bottom edge to side rail's

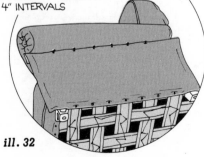

SLIP-TACK OUTSIDE ARM'S BOTTOM EDGE AT 3" INTERVALS; SLIP-TACK ITS FOLDED TOP EDGE AT 4" INTERVALS

ill. 32

bottom with one tack near each leg and one midway between the first two. Then add slip tacks all across side rail's bottom at 3-inch intervals. Smooth fabric up toward inside arm/outside arm junction; fold fabric allowance under at top edge.

Slip-tack outside-arm section's folded top edge to arm rail's outer face at 4-inch intervals. Remove slip tacks from side rail's bottom. Flip outside-arm outer-cover section up over inside arm and blind-tack its top-edge allowance to arm rail's outer face, as directed on page 64. Remove slip tacks from section's top edge.

4 Cut a cardboard tacking strip as long as outside arm's width. Tack it into position over outside-arm outer-cover section's top-edge allowance, as directed on page 65, placing tacks at 2-inch intervals.

5 Cut a burlap section two inches larger than outer perimeter of outside arm (the area bordered by arm rail, side rail, arm post, and back post). Fold one inch of burlap's top edge under; lay fold against arm rail's outer face at inside arm/outside arm junction. Tack burlap's folded edge to arm rail at 2-inch intervals, tacking through underlying cardboard strip and outside-arm outer-cover section's top-edge allowance.

Fold burlap's bottom edge so that fold lies ½ inch shy of side-rail outer face's bottom edge. (Folding edge *over* is easier than tucking it *under*; burlap will be hidden completely by outside-arm outer-cover section eventually.) Tack fold to side rail's outer face at 2-inch intervals.

Fold over and tack burlap's front and rear edges in the same way, with front edge's fold ½ inch shy of arm-post outer face's front edge and rear edge's fold ½ inch shy of back-post outer face's rear edge. (Tack front edge fold from top of burlap to within ½ inch of side rail at bottom.) Trim all folded-over edges to within one inch of tacks.

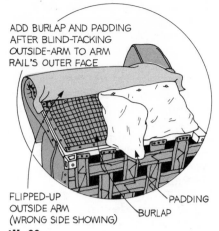

ADD BURLAP AND PADDING AFTER BLIND-TACKING OUTSIDE-ARM TO ARM RAIL'S OUTER FACE

FLIPPED-UP OUTSIDE ARM (WRONG SIDE SHOWING)   PADDING   BURLAP

ill. 33

6 Shape a new layer of cotton padding (see page 66) so that its top edge meets inside arm/outside arm junction, its bottom edge reaches chair bottom (or skirt's top-edge height, if skirt is to be added), and its front and rear edges just cover arm and back posts' outer faces. Tack top of padding to arm rail's outer face (over burlap, cardboard strip, and outer-cover section's top-edge allowance) at 6-inch intervals. Tease padding fibers over tacks or place small wads of padding in tack hollows, so no indentations show where tacks are driven in. Front, rear, and bottom edges of padding need no tacking.

7 Bring outside-arm outer-cover section down over padding. Pull fabric taut and slip-tack section's bottom edge to side rail's bottom with one tack, placed midway between chair's legs. Pull taut and slip-tack section's bottom edge with one tack placed in side rail's bottom, three inches in from front leg. Add slip-tacks at 2-inch intervals between the first two slip tacks. Place all tacks at least one inch in from side rail's outer bottom edge (later, the dustcatcher will be tacked along this margin).

Pull outside-arm section's front-edge allowance taut around arm post's front. Slip-tack allowance to arm post's front with one tack placed three inches up from leg top and another at outside-arm section's top corner, making sure front edge is smooth along arm post and weave is straight along edge. Add tacks at 1-inch intervals to fill space between first two slip tacks. Drive slip tacks in.

8 To fit outside-arm outer-cover section around front leg top, start a cut into outside-arm section's bottom edge at a point

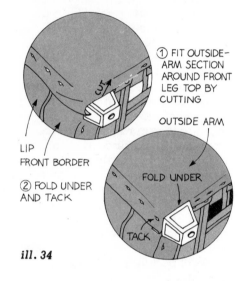

① FIT OUTSIDE-ARM SECTION AROUND FRONT LEG TOP BY CUTTING

OUTSIDE ARM

LIP
FRONT BORDER

② FOLD UNDER AND TACK

FOLD UNDER

TACK

ill. 34

midway between leg outer face's front and rear edges. End cut at top rear corner of leg's outer face, with shears just touching side rail's bottom. Fold under the bottom-allowance flap to front of cut, so fold just meets leg top. Pull folded edge taut around arm post's front and tack to arm post's front just above leg (front edge of outside-arm outer-cover section will now be tacked down whole length of arm post's front).

9 Pull outside-arm outer-cover section's bottom edge taut at rear; slip-tack it to side rail's bottom with one tack, placed three inches in from back leg. Add slip tacks, placed at 2-inch intervals, to fill space between center and rear slip tacks.

Pull rear-edge allowance of outside-arm section taut around back post's back. Slip-tack allowance to back post's back with one tack placed three inches up from leg top and another at section's top corner, making sure rear edge is smooth along back post. Add tacks at 1-inch intervals to fill space between first two slip tacks. Drive slip tacks in.

10 To fit outside-arm outer-cover section around back leg, start a cut into section's bottom edge at a point midway between leg outer face's front and rear edges. End cut at top front corner of leg's outer face, with shears just touching side rail's bottom. Fold under the bottom-allowance flap to rear of cut so fold just meets leg top. Pull folded edge taut around back post's back and tack to back post's back just above leg.

11 Pull remaining three inches of outside-arm outer-cover section's bottom edge at front and rear of side rail taut, folding under triangular flaps of excess at junctions of side rail's bottom with front and back legs. Slip-tack them to side rail's bottom with two tacks at each end. Double-check your work on entire outside-arm outer-cover section. If satisfied, drive all slip tacks in along side rail's bottom.

Repeat the entire installation process on opposite arm with other outside-arm outer-cover section.

Step by step: Putting new outer cover, burlap, and padding on a fully upholstered armchair's outside back

Your chair's outside back is the last major outer-cover section you attach. You must blind-stitch its sides to the outside arms and to the vertical portions of the visible back boxing.

1 Set chair's front on floor, resting the inside back on an up-

CLEAN CLOTH

SET CHAIR ON ITS FRONT ON FLOOR BEFORE STARTING TO WORK ON OUTSIDE BACK
ill. 35

holsterer's horse to keep chair from tipping forward.

2 Trim rear edges of outside-arm outer-cover sections to within ½ inch of tacks along back posts' backs.

3 If your chair has coil springs secured to burlap in its back, and you had to untack the burlap's side edges to reach inside-arm and inside-back stretchers (when stripping old fabric as directed on page 60), now is the time to resecure the old burlap's sides. Pull burlap taut and tack its side edges to back post's backs at 2-inch intervals. Fold side allowances over first line of tacks on each back post and tack again. If your chair has back slats, this step should be unnecessary, because old burlap should have been left completely secured over springs.

4 If your chair had webbing on its outside back, you may have had to remove it while stripping (as directed on page 60). Now is the time to reweb your outside back, using the stretching and tacking techniques given on page 98. Webbing should consist of horizontal strips only, one tacked over each side-to-side row of springs.

5 Trim visible-back-boxing section's rear side and top edges to within ½ inch of tacks on back posts' backs and top rail's back.

PAD SEATS

The simplest of all furniture to reupholster is the chair or stool with a springless seat, known as a "pad seat." A pad seat's base may be closed—made of solid wood—or open—made of webbing. It may or may not be removable. A separate base is usually held in place by screws underneath the chair; to remove the base, simply unscrew it.

A closed seat often only needs to have its outer cover replaced. (If possible, remove the seat base first.) Remove the old cover carefully, noting how it was pleated or cut to fit around arm posts, back posts, and legs, or to fit smoothly over a removable seat base.

An open seat may need to have its limp or rotted webbing stripped. New webbing should then be installed as directed on page 98. Replacing webbing means replacing the burlap that blankets it—page 106 shows how to add new burlap or resecure the old burlap to the chair frame.

If your furniture's old stuffings have a musty odor, you'll want to replace them, too. See page 109 for instructions on how to work with stuffings, and page 108 for information on edge rolls (if your furniture has one). Or save yourself time by layering cotton padding on your pad seat to match the former stuffing's height and contours. Build out as you build up until the next-to-top layer of cotton reaches the seat's edge (see "Crowning" on page 110 for information on this process).

On seats without removable bases, shape the top layer of padding so that it drapes halfway down the seat rails; it need not be tacked to the rails. (The outer cover *will* be tacked to the rails, completely covering the padding.)

Once the stuffing is in position, the new outer cover can be installed. If the fabric you've selected has large dominant motifs or stripes, be sure you've centered a motif or stripe on the outer-cover fabric section before cutting the section out. Replicate the old cover's pleats and/or cuts as closely as possible, to make the new cover fit smoothly.

Even if your furniture originally displayed neither gimp nor double welt, you may wish to add one of these decorative borders to the new outer cover. Page 54 shows how to make double welt; page 87 shows how to install both types of borders. Decorative tacks—available at fabric shops—are a third type of trim. Secure the outer cover with upholsterer's tacks underneath the seat base where the tacks won't show, then edge the cover with a display border of decorative tacks.

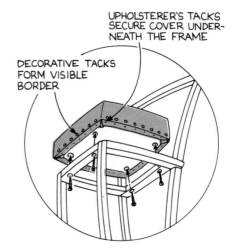

UPHOLSTERER'S TACKS SECURE COVER UNDERNEATH THE FRAME

DECORATIVE TACKS FORM VISIBLE BORDER

---

6 Make welt to extend around perimeter of outside back from one back leg top, up back post's back, over top rail's back, down other back post's back to other back leg top (to make welt, see page 53). Prepare welt ends as directed on page 65.

Slip-tack one end of welt to back post's back just at leg top, using one tack. Position welt seam allowance on back post so that welt cord juts a tiny bit beyond outer edge of back post's back. Align welt and pull it taut up length of back post and slip-tack it to top of back post's back so that welt cord juts above back boxing by a tiny bit, using one tack.

Bend welt to turn corner, making a small pleat in welt seam allowance to take in fullness at corner and slip-tack it, pulled taut, at either end of top rail's back. Bend it around opposite corner (again pleating the allowance) and slip-tack it with one tack to top of opposite back post's back. Run welt down second back post's back as you ran it up the first's, pulling it taut, and slip-tack welt's other end just at leg top.

Add slip tacks at 2-inch intervals to fill space between initial slip tacks. Then drive all slip tacks in.

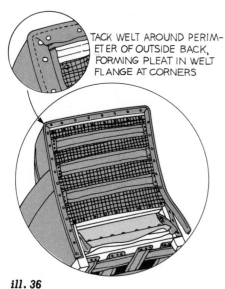

TACK WELT AROUND PERIMETER OF OUTSIDE BACK, FORMING PLEAT IN WELT FLANGE AT CORNERS

ill. 36

7 Place outside-back outer-cover section in position on outside back of chair so allowances extend evenly over its front, rear, top, and bottom edges. Check to make sure any dominant motifs are centered correctly and that fabric's weave is straight. Slip-tack outside-back section's bottom edge to back rail's bottom with one tack near each leg and one midway between the first two. Then add slip tacks all across back rail's bottom at 3-inch intervals. Smooth fabric up toward welt at top of top rail's back; fold fabric allowance under at top edge so folded edge fits snugly up against welt cord when outside-back section is pulled up tautly.

Slip-tack outside-back section's folded top edge to top rail's back at 4-inch intervals. Remove slip tacks from back rail's bottom. Flip outside-back section up over back boxing and blind-tack its

top-edge allowance to top rail's back as directed on page 65. Remove slip tacks from section's top edge.

8 Cut a cardboard tacking strip as long as outside back's width at top edge just beneath welt cord. Tack it into position over outside-back outer-cover section's top-edge allowance, as directed on page 65, placing tacks at 2-inch intervals.

9 Cut a burlap section two inches larger than outer perimeter of outside back (the area bordered by back posts, top rail, and back rail). Fold and tack burlap into place as directed for outside-arm burlap in Step 5, page 77, tacking outside-back burlap to backs of back posts, top rail, and back rail.

10 Shape a new layer of cotton padding (see page 66) so that its top edge meets outside back's top edge just beneath welt cord, its bottom edge reaches chair bottom (or skirt's top-edge height, if skirt is to be added), and its side edges just meet inner edge of welt cord on back posts' backs. Tack padding into place as directed for outside-arm padding in Step 6, page 77. Side and bottom edges need no tacking.

11 Bring outside-back outer-cover section down over burlap, webbing, and padding. Pull fabric taut and slip-tack section's bottom edge to back rail's bottom with one tack, placed midway between chair's back legs. Then tauten fabric and tack section's bottom edge to back rail's bottom with one tack placed three inches in from each back leg.

Fold under section's left side edge so that fold lies over welt seam-allowance flange and fits snugly up against welt cord. Slip-tack section's folded edge, starting at back-post back's top and ending four inches above leg top, at 3-inch intervals.

Pull outside-back section taut across chair's back and fold and

slip-tack its other side edge as you did the first.

12 To fit outside-back outer-cover section around back leg, start a cut into section's bottom edge, cutting upward from center of back leg's back until shears touch back rail's bottom at junction with back leg's inner face. Fold under the excess flap of fabric at section's bottom edge—the portion on leg side of cut—so fold just meets leg top. Slip-tack fold to back post's back with two tacks placed horizontally above leg top. Fold under triangular flap of excess—the portion on rail side of cut—so fold abuts back leg's inner face. Tack fold to back rail's bottom with one or two tacks. Repeat Step 12 above opposite back leg.

13 At the top right-hand corner of outside back, prepare to begin blind-stitching outside-back outer-cover section's side edge to visible-back-boxing and outside-arm outer covers. Cut a length of upholsterer's twine or heavy-duty polyester thread and knot it, as directed on page 65. Then, still following directions on that page and examining illustration 7, blind-stitch section's edge to adjoining sections. Alternating stitches between secured and unsecured sections and passing needle under the intervening welt cord, blind-stitch the entire length of outside-back section's side edge. End the blind-stitching as directed on page 66.

Repeat blind-stitching process on outside-back section's other side edge. Remove slip tacks from along outside-back section's side edges as you stitch.

14 Drive in all slip tacks holding outside-back outer-cover section's bottom edge to back rail's bottom. Add tacks at 1-inch intervals to fill remaining space along back rail's bottom, to secure section's bottom edge to back rail.

Step by step: Putting new outer cover on a fully upholstered armchair's front arm panels

These small, fabric-covered pieces of wood hide the raw front edges of the inside-arm, outside-arm, and front-border outer-cover sections. You use smaller tacks (#2) or staples (¼ inch) to attach the fabric to the front arm panels than you use to attach outer-cover sections to the chair's frame.

1 Lay chair on its back on the floor, arm fronts facing up.

2 Remove old tacks and strip old outer-cover fabric from both front arm panels. Hammer out any old finishing nails used to affix the panels to arm posts.

3 Lay a panel, right side up, on a table or other working surface. Align old padding correctly or replace old padding with new, shaping the new padding as directed on page 66. Position new

THESE SIX DRAWINGS SHOW YOU HOW
TO COVER FRONT ARM PANELS

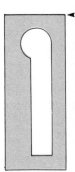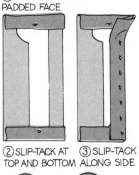

① TURN PANEL ONTO ITS
PADDED FACE

② SLIP-TACK AT ③ SLIP-TACK
TOP AND BOTTOM ALONG SIDE

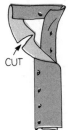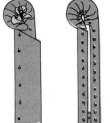

CUT

④ SLIP-TACK ⑤ FORM AND ⑥ ADD TACKS AT
AND CUT TACK PLEATS 1″ INTERVALS; TRIM

ill. 37

front-arm-panel outer-cover section over padding so fabric's pattern is centered as you wish. Holding section in position over panel, turn panel over onto its padded face.

Pull front-arm-panel section's top and bottom edges over wood's top and bottom edges, pulling fabric taut. Slip-tack them to wood with one slip tack each, placed at center of edge.

Pull section's side edge over wood panel's longer straight side edge and slip-tack it at 2-inch intervals just to point where panel's top curve begins. Pull section's other side edge tautly over panel's shorter straight side edge and slip-tack it at 2-inch intervals, stopping three inches short of curve.

At top of wood panel's shorter straight side, where curve suddenly bulges outward, make a cut into front-arm-panel section's side edge, starting the cut about ½ inch below point where curve begins and cutting upward diagonally, aiming shears at point where curve begins. Cut should end just when shears touch wood panel at point where curve begins. Pull fabric below cut taut over straight portion of side edge below curve; slip-tack raw edge in place.

4 Check to see that front-arm-panel outer-cover section's weave is straight on panel's padded side. Then lay panel, padded side down, on work surface again and form front-arm-panel section's top edge into pleats around panel's curved top to take in all excess fullness (to form pleats, consult page 64). Keep checking to be sure weave stays straight on panel's right side as you form and tack pleats.

5 When pleats have been formed and panel looks satisfactory, add tacks between slip tacks at 1-inch intervals along all sides. Drive all slip tacks in. Trim fabric edges to within ½ inch of tacks.

6 Prepare welt to run from one bottom corner of panel, up around panel's top curve, and down to other bottom corner (to make welt, see page 53). Prepare welt ends as directed on page 65.

With panel still lying on its padded face, align one welt end with one bottom corner of panel's back, so welt cord juts over

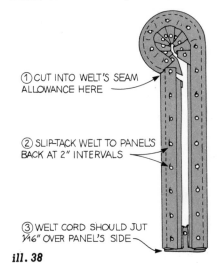

① CUT INTO WELT'S SEAM ALLOWANCE HERE

② SLIP-TACK WELT TO PANEL'S BACK AT 2″ INTERVALS

③ WELT CORD SHOULD JUT 1/16″ OVER PANEL'S SIDE

ill. 38

panel's side. Slip-tack welt to panel's back at 2-inch intervals, aligning it up the side as you go. As you reach curve's base—at top of panel's shorter straight side—make a cut into welt's seam allowance to allow it to round the curve more smoothly. Continue slip-tacking until welt's other end is tacked to panel's other bottom corner.

Add tacks at 1-inch intervals. Drive all slip tacks in.

7 Turn a front arm panel over, padded side up. Lay panel in position along arm front so curve of panel corresponds to curve of arm front and panel's bottom edge meets leg top. Drive 1½-inch finishing nails into panel at 6-inch intervals in a vertical line running down center of panel. Nails should go right through outer-cover fabric, underlying padding,

and panel's wood to penetrate chair's arm front. Before hammering nails all the way in, place a piece of cardboard over outer-cover fabric to prevent hammer from damaging the new outer cover.

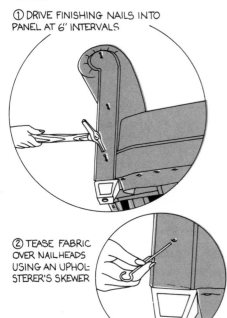

① DRIVE FINISHING NAILS INTO PANEL AT 6" INTERVALS

② TEASE FABRIC OVER NAILHEADS USING AN UPHOLSTERER'S SKEWER

ill. 39

If nail heads are still visible after hammering, depressing outer-cover fabric slightly, use an upholsterer's skewer to tease fabric over nail heads, covering them.

Repeat Steps 1–7 on other front arm panel.

Step by step: Putting new dustcatcher on a fully upholstered armchair

You attach this lightweight fabric section to the bottom of your chair to keep bits of stuffing from drifting down onto your carpet or floor. Once the dustcatcher is in place, you have completed the entire reupholstering process.

1 Turn chair upside down on upholsterer's horses.

2 Cut a section of lightweight fabric one inch larger than outer perimeter of chair's bottom (the area bordered by chair's bottom rails). This section is your dustcatcher.

Lay section on chair's bottom. At chair's front, fold one inch of dustcatcher's front edge under, aligning fold so that it just covers front border's tacked bottom edge on front rail's bottom. Slip-tack fold to front rail's bottom with one tack placed two inches from left front leg, one placed midway between legs, and one placed two inches from right front leg. Add slip tacks every two inches between the initial tacks, placing all tacks close to fold's edge.

Repeat the folding and slip-tacking on dustcatcher's side edge, between left front leg and left back leg.

3 To fit dustcatcher around left front leg, you must make a cut into dustcatcher's left front corner.

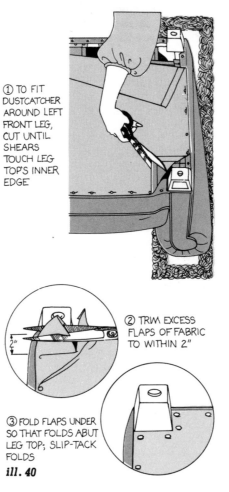

① TO FIT DUSTCATCHER AROUND LEFT FRONT LEG, CUT UNTIL SHEARS TOUCH LEG TOP'S INNER EDGE

② TRIM EXCESS FLAPS OF FABRIC TO WITHIN 2"

③ FOLD FLAPS UNDER SO THAT FOLDS ABUT LEG TOP; SLIP-TACK FOLDS

ill. 40

Letting corner flap of fabric lie against inner edge of chair leg (the edge between leg's inner and back faces), start cut into very corner tip of fabric. Cut downward, at a diagonal to front and side rails, just until shears touch leg top at leg's inner edge. (If your chair's legs are round, make your cuts "Y"-shaped, ending the "Y's" stem one inch shy of leg and then cutting 1-inch-long arms whose span equals leg's diameter. When you fit the cut fabric around leg, tuck triangular center flap of "Y" under.)

On either side of cut, trim off triangular excess flaps of fabric to within two inches of leg top. Fold remaining two inches of flap under on either side of leg so folds abut leg top. Slip-tack folds to front and side rails' bottoms with two tacks each.

4 Fold under and slip-tack dustcatcher's remaining two edges as you did the first two. Fit dustcatcher around remaining three legs as you fit it around the first in Step 3.

Drive all slip tacks in. Dustcatcher is now finished. Before removing your chair from the upholsterer's horses, walk around it and inspect it carefully once more, looking closely at all spots where edges of outer-cover sections are joined to each other or to the frame. Any slip tacks that you overlooked should either be removed (if they are tacked into visible parts of the chair) or driven in.

Any cushions you planned should be assembled now (see page 87), and if you planned a skirt, now is the time to add it (see page 92).

Re-covering variations

Perhaps an attached-cushion ottoman accompanies your chair. Or maybe your furniture has wings, a barrelback, or an open-arm antique design whose crowned tight back and seat require double welt or gimp to hide the outer-cover fabric's edges where they meet the wood frame. The following instructions will give re-covering techniques specific to these furniture variations. Before you begin on them, be sure you've read through this chapter's preceding pages; much of the preceding information probably also applies to your furniture.

Attached-cushion ottoman

Upholstering your attached-cushion ottoman may well take less time than did the shaping and sewing of its cover.

Start by laying 4-inch-wide strips of new padding along the edges of the wooden base's top to

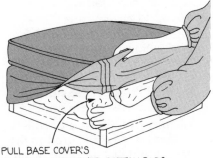

4" WIDE PADDING STRIPS SHOULD OVERHANG OTTOMAN BASE'S EDGE ROLL BY 1/4"

ill. 41

conceal and pad them. Lay the new padding over any old padding unless the old padding is disintegrating; if necessary, replace the old padding entirely (see page 66). Each strip should be as long as one edge of the ottoman, and should be aligned along the edge so that the strip's outer edge overhangs the base's edge roll by 1/4 inch. Where two strips overlap at one of the ottoman's corners, tear off the end of one strip so that it abuts but no longer overlaps the other strip's end. Repeat this on each other corner so that the strips no longer overlap each other, but still rim the ottoman's edges in a continuous single layer.

Blanket these strips with a rectangle of new padding large enough to extend down the base's sides to within two inches of the base outer cover's bottom-edge level. Tear off the triangular flaps of excess padding that jut out at the four corners so that the corners won't bulge when you put the outer cover on.

Place the covered cushion, with its top face down, on the ottoman's padded wooden base. If the top cushion face's edges ride more than two inches above the base's padding, remove some padding from the middle of the base's top, to lower the cushion slightly. (Otherwise, the ottoman will look overstuffed.)

Remove the cushion from the wooden base. Pull the base outer cover (attached to the bottom cushion face) over the cushion boxing, wrong side out (see illustration 42). Now flip the cushion so

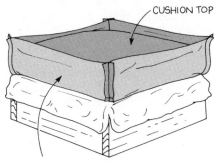

CUSHION TOP

PULL BASE'S OUTER COVER UP OVER CUSHION BOXING, WRONG SIDE OUT

ill. 42

its top face is up and place it on the ottoman's padded wooden base. Place an extra cotton pad over each of the wooden base's corners, where the base outer cover's side seams will lie. Press-

ing a pad tightly against the base corner with one hand, pull a base outer cover's corner down over it (see illustration 43).

Repeat this on the remaining three corners—be sure that the seams at the outer cover's corners fall exactly over the wooden base's corners. Slip-tack the base outer cover's bottom edge at 2-inch intervals to the frame sides' outer faces, one inch up from the base outer cover's bottom edges. Scrutinize your work, then drive the slip tacks in.

To secure the ottoman's border outer cover to the wooden base, follow Steps 1–4 on page 94; the border is blind-tacked into position as you would a skirt.

Then position and tack a new layer of border padding as directed for the front-border outer cover in Step 5 on page 73. Pull the ottoman's border outer cover down and slip-tack its bottom edge to the wooden base's bottom, making cuts to fit it around the base's legs (if any) as you would a front-border outer-cover section (see Steps 6–7 on page 74).

Scrutinize your work; drive in all tacks but those within three inches of each corner. Form the excess fabric at the corners into pleats (see page 64) and finish tacking the bottom edge of the border outer cover to the wooden base's bottom.

Add a dustcatcher to your ottoman's underside, following the directions on page 82.

Open-arm antique with crowned back and seat

If your chair resembles the chair pictured in the Measurement List on page 43, the following tips will help you to reupholster it.

Work on the chair's seat first. Once you've peeled off the seat's old outer-cover fabric, shape a fresh layer of padding to reach to the bottom of the rails (see page

PULL BASE COVER'S CORNERS DOWN OVER COTTON PADS

ill. 43

66). Lay the new padding over the old padding (or replace the old padding entirely, if necessary).

Position the new seat outer-cover section on the chair (centering any dominant motifs or stripes), then slip-tack it to the rails' bottoms on all sides, using three tacks on each side (one about three inches away from each leg and one midway between them). Now fold the seat section's four corners back over themselves, wrong side out, so that the folds just touch the nearest back or arm post. Make a cut into each folded corner, cutting from the corner's tip straight toward the back or arm post, and stopping ⅛ inch from each post.

Smooth the cut corners around each post and trim the triangular-shaped flaps on either side of each cut to within 1½ inches of the posts. Fold the resulting raw edges under so that each fold abuts the nearest post edge; then slip-tack the folded edges to the rails' outside faces with tacks placed vertically at the rails' ends, parallel to the posts. To the seat section's bottom edge, slip-tacked to the rails' bottoms, add slip tacks at 1-inch intervals, pleating wherever necessary to smooth the fabric around curved frame members (see page 64). Survey your work; drive all slip tacks in.

Secure the chair's inside-back outer-cover section much as you secured its seat. You must make a "Y"-shaped cut into the side edges of the section where they meet the arm rails—the stem of the "Y" should end just short of the rail and the "Y's" arms should be one inch long, spanning the diameter of the rail. Pull the fabric on either side of the cut around the arm rail; tuck the triangular flap of excess between the "Y's" arms under so the fold sits against the arm rail, then pull the section's side edges above and below the cut around to the

chair's back for tacking. You'll also need to make cuts in the inside-back section's bottom edge to fit the fabric around each back post just as you made cuts in the seat section to fit it around the posts. As you pull the inside-back section's edges around to the chair's back and tack them at 1-inch intervals, pleat them wherever necessary to keep the fabric smooth around the frame's curves.

To secure the outside-back outer-cover section, along with its burlap and padding, follow the guidelines suggested for the outside wing (page 86), blind-stitching around all edges, beginning with its curved top edge.

Add double welt or gimp (see page 87) to border all the wood/fabric junctions on the chair (trim should cover the tacks holding the seat's fabric edges next to the posts).

Fully upholstered barrel-back chair with back slats and tight seat

The following method of reupholstering a barrelback requires that your furniture have a back slat, rising from the arm liner to the arm rail, parallel to and 1½ inches away from each back post, between the back post and the arm post.

If your barrelback does not now have back slats, you can fashion them from 1 by 2 lengths of wood, cut to fit tightly between the arm liner and arm rail, 1½ inches from the back post. Glue them in place with aliphatic resin glue, also called "yellow glue." The 1-inch faces of the slats should become the slats' inner and outer faces.

After the glue dries, add a 1-inch finishing nail at each slat's top and bottom, driving the nails in from the chair's outside arm on a diagonal through the slat and into the arm rail or arm liner.

A fully upholstered barrelback, such as that pictured in the Measurement List on page 43, is reupholstered in the same sequence, using similar techniques,

as the fully upholstered armchair described on pages 67–82, with the following major exceptions.

1. A barrelback's T-shaped tight seat must be pleated at its front corners (see page 64 and illustration 4). It also should have a bottom stretcher sewn to its rear edge, to be used in tacking the seat section's rear edge to the back rail.

2. Padding for the inside arms should cover the front faces of the arm posts, and should be slid between the back slats and back posts to reach but not cover the outer faces of the back slats. The inside-arm padding's top edge should extend over the arm rail's top to the inside arm/outside arm junction. The padding for the inside back should just reach but not cover the outer faces of the back posts.

3. The inside-arm outer-cover sections should have stretchers sewn to their rear and bottom edges. The inside-back outer-cover section should have stretchers sewn to its bottom and both its side edges.

4. Install the inside-back outer-cover section before you install the inside-arm sections.

5. Slide each inside-arm rear-edge stretcher between the back slat and the back post, pulling the inside-arm section taut over the back slat, but tack the stretcher to the back post's back, on top of the inside back's side stretcher.

Stuff wads of padding between the slat and the post, while standing at the chair's rear, until the inside-arm outer cover is pushed against the inside-back outer cover, closing any gap between the slat and the post which could be seen from the front of the chair. The outside-arm burlap will keep the padding wads in place.

6. Pull the front edges of the wrap-around inside-arm outer-cover sections around the padded arm posts' fronts and tack them to the arm posts' outer faces. You will have to form a single pleat at each arm post's top, with its outer fold running horizontally around the arm post's front (see page 64), to take in the excess fabric where the arm post meets the arm rail.

7. You must blind-stitch the outside-arm and outside-back outer-cover sections' top edges rather than blind-tack them, just as you would an outside-wing section (see page 86).

Wings

Though several types of wings exist, the most common wing framework consists of a wing rail connecting the furniture's back post with the curved wing post which forms the wing's front edge. This is the type of wing illustrated on the wing chair in the Measurement List on page 44. As shown on page 96, a vertical wing slat sometimes reinforces the assembly.

Outer-cover sections should be installed on wing furniture in the following order: lip/decking section first, followed by the inside arms, front border (if any), inside wings, and inside back. Next, move to the outside wings, outside arms, and finally the outside-back section.

Before beginning to re-cover the wings, be sure you position your wrap-around boxed inside-arm outer-cover sections properly. The rear of the arm boxing should have a "Y"-shaped cut made into it, so that it straddles the wing post smoothly. The arms of the "Y" should be one inch long, and should span just the thickness of the wing post. Tack the triangular flap of excess between the "Y's" arms to the front of the wing post. Tack the outer rear

portion of the arm boxing to the outer face of the wing post with two tacks, placed an inch apart. Also tack the arm boxing's outer rear portion to the arm rail's outer face below the wing, tacking at 1-inch intervals all the way to the section's rear top corner. Tack the outer rear portion of the arm boxing's welt seam allowance to the arm rail's outer face at 1-inch intervals, over the tacked arm boxing. The welt should eventually abut the outside-wing section's bottom edge. (Later, the outside-arm outer-cover section will conceal the welt's seam allowance.) The inner rear portion of the arm boxing should be tacked to the inner face of the wing post as you tacked the outer portion to the post's outer face, and to the top of the arm rail at 1-inch intervals as far as the inside arm/inside back crevice. Make sure you position all these wing-post tacks as high up on the wing post as the section edges will reach, so that the wing outer-cover sections can cover the tack heads completely.

As you did with the inside arms, plan to work on the inside wings simultaneously, to insure symmetry in their padding, pleating, pulling, and finishing.

First, peel off each inside wing's old outer cover, but leave the old padding in place (unless it must be replaced—see page 66). Shape a new layer of padding to the wing's configuration, using the instructions on page 67. Tuck the new padding's rear edge into the crevice between the inside wing and the inside back. Place the new inside-wing outer-cover section over the padding, making sure that its weave runs straight up and down, and that the correct fabric allowances overhang the frame members on all sides.

Slip-tack the inside-wing section's top edge to the wing rail's outer face with one tack at its center and one at each end. Pull the front end of the welt sewn to the inside-wing section's bottom edge down tautly and around the wing post's front to the wing post's outer

face; slip-tack the section's bottom edge, just above the welt, to the

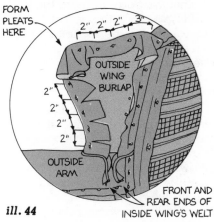

SLIP-TACK INSIDE WING TO WING RAIL, WING POST, AND BACK POST AT 2" INTERVALS

FORM PLEATS HERE

2" 2" 2" 3"

OUTSIDE WING BURLAP

2"
2"
2"
2"

OUTSIDE ARM

FRONT AND REAR ENDS OF INSIDE WING'S WELT

ill. 44

post's outer face with one tack. Push the welt's rear end through the inside wing/inside back crevice, along the back post's inner face to the furniture's outside back. Standing at the furniture's rear, pull the welt's rear end down tautly and slip-tack the inside-wing section's bottom edge, just above the welt, to the back post's back with one tack (see illustration 44). The slip-tacked inside-wing section's bottom edge should hide the tacks holding the arm boxing to the wing post.

Keeping the inside-wing section's weave straight up and down, pull the section's front edge around to the wing post's outer face. Cut into the section's lower front-edge allowance every two inches so that you can fit the section snugly to the post's lower, concave curve. Slip-tack the flaps of allowance to the post's outer face at 2-inch intervals, checking to be sure the section rounds the post's curve smoothly. To fit the section's upper front-edge allowance smoothly around the wing post's upper, convex curve, pleat the fabric excess (see page 64).

Now remove the three initial slip tacks placed at the wing rail's top. With your palms, smooth the inside-wing section up over the padding, starting at the bottom welt. Press the section's fabric against the padding near the padding's top with one hand while you pull the section taut and slip-tack its top edge at 2-inch intervals to the wing rail's outer face. Stop tacking three inches from the back post.

To fit the inside-wing outer-cover section's rear edge around the top rail at the chair's back, you must make a cut, using the following instructions. Fold the inside-wing section's rear-edge allowance back, wrong side out, over the inside wing. Slide your fingers under the fold about ¼ of the way down from the wing's top, at the level of the top rail's bottom, and push the fold through the inside wing/inside back crevice until you feel the back post through the fabric with your fingertips. Keeping your hand in

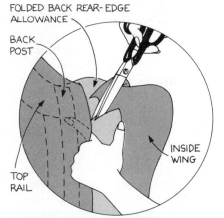

FOLDED BACK REAR-EDGE ALLOWANCE

BACK POST

INSIDE WING

TOP RAIL

CUT INTO INSIDE WING'S REAR-EDGE ALLOWANCE IN ORDER TO FIT IT AROUND TOP RAIL
ill. 45

that position as a guide, cut into the folded-over allowance's edge until your shears reach the crevice (as in illustration 45). Marking the spot where the fold touched the back post, pull the fold of the inside-wing section's rear-edge allowance back out of the crevice. Deepen the cut until it is one inch shy of the spot where the fold

touched the post. Then cut 1-inch-long arms to form a "Y"-shaped cut (the distance between the arms should approximate the back post's width).

Push the portion of the section's rear edge located below the cut through the inside wing/inside back crevice, along the back post's inner face. Pull it taut and slip-tack it to the back post's back at 2-inch intervals. Pull the portion of the section's rear edge located above the cut over the furniture's top rail; slip-tack it to the back post's back near the top with one tack. If the fabric bunches up as it is pulled over the top rail, snip into the fabric edge to release and smooth the fabric over the top rail.

Slip-tack the inside-wing section's edges all along the outer faces of the wing post and wing rail at 1-inch intervals. You may need to form the section's edges into more pleats where the post curves to meet the rail, if there is excess fullness remaining there. Scrutinize your work; drive all slip tacks in.

Once you have completed your furniture's inside outer-cover sections, you should be ready to install the outside-wing outer-cover sections.

First, position a rectangle of burlap large enough to cover the outer perimeter of the wing frame members' outer faces on the outside wing. Slip-tack the burlap to the frame's outer faces, ½ inch in from the faces' outer edges, at 2-inch intervals. Trim the outer edges of the burlap to within ½ inch of tacks.

Shape a layer of cotton padding (see page 66) to cover the outer faces of the frame members entirely. Slip-tack it in place at each corner of the wing frame's outer faces; drive the tacks in and, with an upholsterer's skewer, tease the cotton fibers over the tack heads to obscure their imprint in the padding.

Make welt to extend around the perimeter of the outside wing's frame members, preparing one welt end as directed on

page 65. Beginning with the prepared welt end, tack the welt to the outside wing's frame, from the bottom of the wing post up over the wing rail to the back post's top, following the outside-back outer-cover directions in Step 6 on page 79. Stop three inches short of the unprepared welt end and rip open the last inch of welt casing. Cut off the last inch of cord; fold the casing closed again, pull it around the back post's outer face, and tack the empty casing end to the back post's back with one tack.

Slip-tack the rectangular outside-wing outer-cover section to the wing frame members' outer faces over the burlap and padding, making sure that the weave is straight and any dominant motifs or stripes are correctly centered. Chalk the outline of the outside wing's configuration on the outside-wing section, tracing just along the inside of the welt. Remove the slip tacks; take the section off the chair and trim it to within ½ inch of the chalk line.

Folding the section's allowances under as you go, align and slip-tack the outside-wing section on the outside wing at 1-inch intervals, beginning with the top edge. Align the folded edges of the outside-wing section so that the front and top folds abut the welt tacked to the wing rail and post. (The folded allowances should form their own natural pleats along the section's curved edges.) Align the outside-wing section's folded bottom-edge allowance so it abuts the arm boxing's rear welt. Do not fold the section's rear edge; instead, pull it around the back post's outer face and slip-tack it to the back post's back at 2-inch intervals.

Blind-stitch the outside-wing section along the wing post and wing rail to the inside-wing section under the welt cord (see pages 65–66). Blind-stitch the section's bottom edge to the outside-arm section under the welt cord, after outside-arm section is installed. Remove the slip tacks from the back post's back. Pull the section's rear edge taut and tack it to the back post again at 1-inch intervals, driving the tacks all the way in.

Double welt and gimp

Unlike single welt, which is sewn to the fabric section it borders, or is permanently tacked against the fabric's edge, double welt and gimp are both glued into position on your furniture. They are used to hide exposed tacks or staples and to conceal the junction of fabric and wood on upholstered furniture whose wood frame is exposed. You might use one or the other of them simply to give your furniture a finished look. To do the job, you'll need a squeeze bottle of liquid polyvinyl acetate, called "white glue;" #3 tacks; a tack hammer; and shears.

To prepare double welt for gluing, trim its allowance to within 1/8 inch of the welt cords. At one end of the welt, rip open 3/4 inch of the seam and snip off 3/4 inch of both cords.

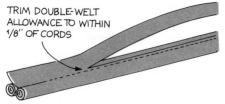

TRIM DOUBLE-WELT ALLOWANCE TO WITHIN 1/8" OF CORDS

ill. 46

Gimp needs no special preparation for gluing.

Take the precaution of covering with a clean rag any new upholstery in the vicinity of your gluing process. Set one end of the gimp or welt against the furniture so that the empty 3/4 inch of welt casing or an extra 3/4 inch of gimp extends beyond the spot where you want the trim to begin. It's a good idea to begin and end trim at inconspicuous parts of your furniture such as the bottom of its inside back, or its rear.

Fold the extra 3/4 inch of trim end under and hold it against the furniture while you flip the rest of the trim out of the way.

Now tack the trim to the frame 3/4 inch in from the trim's end (in other words, place the tack right where you eventually want the trim to begin on your furniture). Squirt a narrow band of glue, six

SQUIRT A 6" BAND OF GLUE DOWN MIDDLE OF TRIM'S WRONG SIDE

2"

SLIP-TACK EVERY 2"

ill. 47

inches long, down the middle of the trim's wrong side, starting it right at the tack. Fold the trim back over the tack to hide it and press the glued trim surface against the junction of the outer-cover section and the frame's wood, hiding the edges of both (see illustration 47). Place a slip tack through the trim where the glue ends. Fill in the glued six inches with slip tacks placed at 2-inch intervals.

Continue gluing and then slip-tacking, doing six inches at a time, as you did the first six inches until you're within three inches of the point where the trim should end. Cut the trim off 3¾ inches beyond the last tack. If you're working with double welt, rip open the last 3/4 inch of its seam and snip 3/4 inch off of both cords (as you did to prepare the welt for gluing). Squirt glue along the wrong side of the trim's last 3¾ inches, and along the right side of its last 3/4 inch. Fold the last 3/4 inch under and press the last of the trim against the junction of the

upholstery and the frame; slip-tack its folded end.

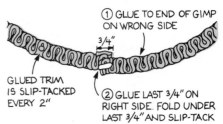

① GLUE TO END OF GIMP ON WRONG SIDE

3/4"

GLUED TRIM IS SLIP-TACKED EVERY 2"

② GLUE LAST 3/4" ON RIGHT SIDE. FOLD UNDER LAST 3/4" AND SLIP-TACK

ill. 48

Remove the slip tacks when the glue has dried (usually half an hour is enough drying time).

Cushions

Though several cushion styles and fillings exist, we will guide you only through the making of the most basic: a loose boxed cushion, filled either with your old cushion's spring unit or with foam (which is more easily inserted). To learn how to make other types of cushions, see the *Sunset* book, *How to Make Pillows.*

Shaping cushion cover sections

In order to insure that your cushion fits snugly, we recommend that you shape your loose cushion's outer cover *after* reupholstering the inside arms and inside back of your furniture. Doing it at that point also enables you to match your deck cushion's stripes or dominant motifs (if it has any) with the newly dressed inside back, or to match a back cushion to the back boxing, if you wish.

Deck-cushion cover sections. The following steps show how to shape the outer cover for a fully upholstered armchair's loose deck cushion.

Step 1: Label a cushion face "top"; place it, right side up, on chair's deck. Smooth fabric out to deck edges, making sure motifs or

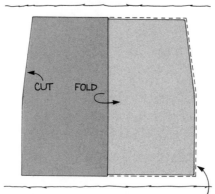

① HOLD CHALK VERTICALLY TO TRACE SIDE AND REAR EDGES OF CUSHION FACE

② RUN CHALK'S SIDE ALONG LIP'S FRONT EDGE TO TRACE FRONT EDGE OF CUSHION FACE

ill. 49

stripes are in line with those on the inside back. Holding chalk vertically, trace side and rear edges of cushion face, letting your hand brush along inside arms and inside back as you trace. Trace cushion face's front edge by running chalk's side along front edge of lip.

Step 2: Place cushion face on a flat surface. Adjust chalk line to make face halves symmetrical. If differences between outlines on either half are considerable, repeat Step 1. To create symmetry and make your cushion reversible, you may have to repad and retack the inside back (see page 74) or an inside arm (see page 70).

Step 3: Chalk ½-inch seam allowance on all sides of cushion face.

Step 4: To allow for a spring cushion's puffiness, make a chalk mark ¼ inch outside the seam allowance line on cushion's left

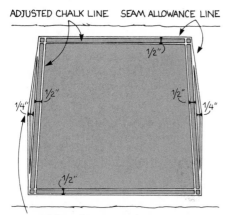

ADJUSTED CHALK LINE   SEAM ALLOWANCE LINE

½"

½"   ½"

¼"   ¼"

½"

CHALK ¼" OUTSIDE SEAM ALLOWANCE LINE TO ALLOW FOR SPRING CUSHION'S PUFFINESS

ill. 50

side, midway between rear and front edges. (If your cushion will be stuffed with foam, make the mark only ⅛ inch outside seam allowance line.) Connect the mark to front and back corners with a gradual curve (see illustration 51). Repeat mark and curve on other side.

Step 5: Starting at mid-front and continuing along one side to mid-back, cut out half of cushion face. Be sure to snip along outer curved—not inner straight—chalk line. Fold cushion face in half. Cut out face's second half, using the first as a guide.

CUT   FOLD

CUT OUT HALF OF CUSHION FACE, FOLD OVER, USE FIRST HALF AS GUIDE TO CUT OUT SECOND HALF

ill. 51

Step 6: From each of cushion face's front corners, chalk a mark 2½ inches in toward center of front edge and a mark ¼ inch along side edge toward rear. Join ¼-inch mark and 2½-inch mark at each front corner with a convex curved line. Cut along curved lines. Curves give the finished cushion square corners and a straight front, instead of jutting corners and a buckled front. (Don't clip back corners because back edge's slight inward curve helps cushion fit the inside back's contour.)

Step 7: Use shaped top cushion face as pattern to cut the bottom cushion face. Place top face's right side against bottom face's right side. Check motif alignment, then chalk the outline of top face on bottom and cut out bottom face.

If your fabric boasts dominant motifs (or stripes), match front boxing to top cushion face; page

36 tells you how. Cut boxing to correct size. Take care to chalk seam lines on boxing's top and bottom edges to insure an even finished length.

Back-cushion cover sections. Trace, cut, and shape a boxed back cushion as you shaped the deck cushion, outlining the inside back—instead of the deck—on the cushion faces. (If the inside back of your furniture is shaped like the inside back of the fully upholstered armchair, you'll need to snip the fabric at the arm's top curve when outlining the top cushion face's sides, as you did when shaping the fully upholstered armchair's inside back—page 50 tells you how.)

Before tracing a back-cushion face's outline, check whether the finished cushion is to rest directly on the furniture's deck, or on the deck cushion. Then position the bottom edge of the back-cushion face's outer-cover section accordingly, either aligned with the deck or with the top of the deck cushion.

Measure the distance that the top of the back cushion is to extend above the top of the inside back; allow that much extra fabric at the top back-cushion face's top edge when you chalk the outline, before cutting the section out.

Step by step: Sewing cover for a fully upholstered armchair's deck cushion

Sew boxed deck and back-cushion covers in four steps, as follows. (Skip Steps 1 and 4 if you're sewing a cover for an ottoman's attached cushion, and follow the variation on page 90.)

1 First, prepare zipper boxing. Begin by fitting zipper foot onto your sewing machine. Fold under the top inch—wrong sides together—of one of the zipper-boxing outer-cover sections (you cut two). Place folded boxing section—right side up—over zipper so boxing section's folded

edge more than halfway covers zipper teeth. Join boxing section to zipper with ¼-inch seam along fold (see illustration 52).

Fold under the bottom inch of the second zipper-boxing outer-cover section, wrong sides together. Position second boxing

FOLD UNDER TOP 1" OF FIRST ZIPPER BOXING; PLACE SO FOLDED EDGE MORE THAN HALFWAY COVERS ZIPPER TEETH

STITCH ¼" SEAMS

②

SECOND FOLDED EDGE SHOULD SLIGHTLY OVERLAP FIRST. MEASURE TOTAL FINISHED LENGTH

ill. 52

section on zipper's opposite side from first boxing section, so second boxing section's folded edge slightly overlaps the first section's folded edge. Before you continue sewing, measure zipper boxing's total length; it should be the same as front boxing's total length. If it isn't, adjust second zipper-boxing section's fold until front and back boxings are equal lengths and, if necessary, snip excess from second zipper-boxing section's bottom edge.

If you bought a length of zipper from a roll, slip tab on zipper track now. Then turn zipper boxing wrong side up. Cut a 1-inch square of fabric from a cover scrap and place it over zipper teeth, with square's outside edge aligned with zipper boxing's end. Sew ⅜-inch seam along boxing's length at end; repeat with a second 1-inch-square scrap at other end. Fabric squares keep zipper

tab from sliding off its track at either end.

SEW 3/8" SEAM INTO 1" SQUARE OF FABRIC TO KEEP ZIPPER TAB FROM SLIDING OFF

ill. 53

2 Then, prepare welt. Place longest welt strip in middle, and sew welt strips together, end to end, to make a continuous length of welt casing (see page 53). Make casing's length six inches longer than cushion's circumference. Sew cord into welt casing.

3 Next, sew welt to cushion faces. On right side of top cushion face's fabric, align raw edges of welt's and cushion face's seam allowances, placing welt end at center of cushion face's back edge. Starting three inches in from one welt end, sew welt around cushion face until you are within three inches of the point on the cushion face's edge at which you started attaching the welt. Join welt ends as explained on page 90, and finish sewing welt to cushion face. Repeat on bottom cushion face.

4 Finally, sew boxings to cushion faces. Notch top cushion face's front edge at its center. Fold front boxing in half along length; notch fold at top edge. Aligning notches and checking to be sure motifs or nap directions are correctly matched, pin front boxing to top cushion face, right sides together. Starting approximately five inches behind front corner on cushion's right-hand side, sew boxing to front of cushion face, following chalked seam line and stopping five inches beyond corner on cushion's left-hand side.

Pin zipper boxing—all but the last two inches at either

end—to top cushion face's back edge and around rear corners, snipping boxing's seam allowance ½ inch away from each corner and directly *at* each corner, to make boxing turn around corners smoothly. (Don't make snips deep enough to touch seam line—see page 54.)

Leaving five inches of front boxing free at either end, pin unsewn portions of front boxing to top cushion face's sides. Sew one

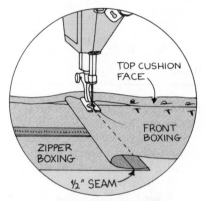

SEW FRONT BOXING END TO ZIPPER BOXING END WITH ½" SEAM. THEN FOLD EXCESS BOXING OVER ZIPPER BOXING, AND SEAM AGAIN

ill. 54

end of front boxing to adjoining end of zipper boxing along boxings' lengths, right sides together, to make ½-inch seam. Fold excess width of front boxing over zipper boxing to take up all slack. Sew second seam as closely as possible over first front boxing/zipper boxing seam, catching overlap of excess front boxing in seam. Repin joined and overlapped boxings to top cushion face.

Overlap and sew opposite ends of front boxing and zipper boxing together in the same way. Then finish sewing boxing to top cushion face.

To sew boxing to bottom cushion face, fold boxing along its length at corners and notch bottom edge at folds. Open zipper enough to turn cover right side out after you finish sewing. Aligning notches in boxing with bottom cushion face's corners, pin bottom face to boxing. With boxing on top, join sections with ½-inch seam sewn along chalk line.

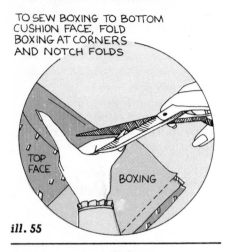

TO SEW BOXING TO BOTTOM CUSHION FACE, FOLD BOXING AT CORNERS AND NOTCH FOLDS

TOP FACE

BOXING

ill. 55

Sewing variation: attached-cushion ottoman. The attached cushion of an ottoman requires some techniques which differ slightly from those for a loose boxed deck or back cushion.

After following Steps 2 and 3 (page 89), make sure one of the longer boxing sections matches the ottoman's top cushion face (as in Step 11 on page 39) if your fabric has dominant motifs or stripes. Fold this longer boxing section in half along its length; notch the top edge at the fold. Join all the boxing section ends to make one continuous circular section. Fold the top cushion face in half along its length; notch the front edge at the fold. Aligning notches and checking for proper matching of motifs or nap direction, pin the boxing, right sides together, to the top cushion face. Make sure that the boxing seams fall exactly at the face's corners; repin them if necessary. With the boxing on top, join the boxing to the cushion face with a ½-inch seam along the chalked seam line.

Fold the boxing along its length at the corners; notch the bottom edge at the folds. Pin the

bottom cushion face to the boxing, leaving space equivalent to a zipper boxing unpinned (see the Measurement List for the fully upholstered armchair on page 41 for the dimension of the zipper boxing). This opening allows you to turn the cushion cover right side out after you finish sewing the boxing to the bottom cushion face with a ½-inch seam along the pinned edges. You blind-stitch the opening shut after filling the cover (see page 92).

Joining welt ends

To join the ends of a continuous length of welt—as you do when encircling your cushions (page 89) and skirt (page 94) with welt—follow this procedure: about three inches before you come to the final welt end, stop sewing the welt to your outer-cover section, backstitch, break the threads, and take the section out from under the needle. (Remember that you also left three inches of the beginning welt end unattached.)

Overlap the two welt ends so that the casings lie flat against the outer-cover section; cut off any excess so the overlap of the ends is two inches long. Take out the last two inches of stitching at both welt ends; push the cords aside. Smooth the welt casing ends toward each other and pin them together so that the casings lie flat against the outer-cover section. Sew the casing ends together, trim the seam allowance to ½ inch, and finger-press the seam open.

Overlap the two welt cord ends so that the cords lie flat against the outer-cover section; cut off any excess so the overlap of the ends is one inch long. Thin the overlapped cord ends by snipping half of the cord's thickness off each end. They should now overlap without creating a big lump at their conjunction. Unravel a few strands from the cord ends and pull the strands toward the welt-casing edges. Fold the welt casing back over the cord ends. Put the outer-cover section back under the needle and finish

sewing the welt to the section, taking care to catch the unravelled cord strands in the seam. The strands caught in the seam will prevent the welt cord ends from sliding apart inside the casing.

Inside the cover

Whether your old cushion got its bounce from springs or from foam, you may wish to replace either old filling with a new polyurethane foam slab. Springs can prove difficult to insert by hand into a new cover (though a professional can do it for you for a fee), and old foam has often disintegrated or grown lumpy. To find polyurethane foam, try checking in fabric shops, or look in the Yellow Pages under "Upholsterer's Supplies." Buy a slab as thick as your cushion boxing's finished length—a softer, squashier grade for back cushions and a firmer one for deck cushions.

You'll also want to purchase unbonded, backed polyester batting (also called "quilted" batting), available precut or by the yard at a fabric shop or upholstery wholesaler. Buy a length of polyester batting for each cushion on your furniture. To determine the length of batting you'll need for each cushion, add the cushion face's length plus the boxing's length; double this amount and add six inches for handling.

Wrapped around springs or foam, this batting gives cushions more cushiness than the bonded variety of polyester batting or cotton padding, and its quilted layer of nonwoven fabric reduces friction between the batting fibers and the cushion's cover fabric, minimizing lumps. Both polyester and cotton fibers will help keep foam from disintegrating, but polyester batting makes the hand-filling of cushions easier than does cotton.

To give a slab of foam its final shape, lay the sewn cover on the slab's top. Trace the cushion face's outline on the foam with a felt pen, ¼ inch outside the welt if the foam is soft, ⅛ inch outside if it's relatively firm. Cut along the outline with a serrated knife, or use an electric carving knife if you have one.

TRACE CUSHION FACE'S OUTLINE ON FOAM WITH A FELT PEN

CUT ALONG OUTLINE WITH A SERRATED KNIFE

ill. 56

Wrap the filling. If you decide to reuse your springs, leave any old hair or moss in place, but replace the top layer of old cotton padding with new padding (see page 66), to rid your new cushion of lumps.

Whichever filling you've chosen—springs or foam—lay it on your length of polyester batting. Roll the filling over once, folding the batting over with it. Allow enough batting to cover the entire filling, plus an extra six inches. Sever any excess batting with shears.

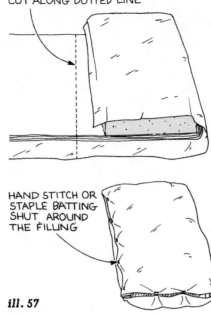

ALLOW ENOUGH BATTING TO COVER ENTIRE CUSHION FILLING, PLUS 6". CUT ALONG DOTTED LINE

HAND STITCH OR STAPLE BATTING SHUT AROUND THE FILLING

ill. 57

Tear the batting fibers away from the edges of the batting to make a ½-inch margin of bare backing on all sides. Fold the bare backing margin over to cover the edge of the remaining fibers. Then hand-stitch or staple the batting shut around the filling, near the part of the filling that will correspond to the seams at the bottom cushion face's back and side edges, working from the center and leaving the two inches nearest the back corners unsewn or unstapled. Then tuck one corner edge of the batting under the other at each of the back corners and finish stapling or sewing those corners, so that the edges overlap smoothly and snugly.

Stuff the cushion. Stuffing takes stamina; rest a moment first. Then zip the boxing open and lay the cushion cover on a flat surface, right side out.

Whether you are using springs or foam as filling, you'll need to fill out the cushion's corners with loose batting. You can do this after stuffing the cushion if you're working with foam. But it's difficult to reach inside a cushion cover once a spring unit is in it.

Before you install your spring unit in a rectangular spring-cushion cover, fill its front corners

with rolls of batting the length of the cushion boxing (you fill the back corners as you zip the cushion shut). See page 92 for the technique of stuffing a T-shaped spring cushion.

To stuff a cushion with foam, fold the wrapped foam in half and grasp it with one hand or under

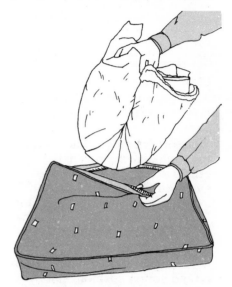

TO STUFF A CUSHION WITH FOAM, FOLD WRAPPED FOAM IN HALF FIRST

ill. 58

one arm. Hold the cover's zipper opening apart with the other hand and shove the folded foam into the cover. Push the foam as far toward the cushion's front as possible, then press the foam down at the center and let go. Push it in to the corners and edges while holding the cover with one hand.

To stuff a spring cushion, hold the cover open and push the wrapped spring unit in, one corner at a time. Ease the cover over

TO STUFF A SPRING CUSHION COVER, PUSH WRAPPED SPRING UNIT IN ONE CORNER AT A TIME

ill. 59

the unit, working it up slowly—first one side and then the other, alternately.

Spring or foam-filled, beat the stuffed cushion with both palms to distribute the filling evenly. Fill out a foam cushion's front corners with loose padding. Fill out the back corners of either kind of cushion with more loose padding as you zip it shut.

You can ease the task of zipping a spring cushion shut by holding the cushion between your knees and pressing down on the springs as you zip.

• **T-shaped spring cushion.** A T-shaped spring cushion's outer cover has "ears" which must be filled with padding, since most spring units are rectangular and fill only the central rectangle of the T-shaped cover. To fill out each "ear," ball up cotton padding to make a 10 to 12-inch square of padding. Then push the square's smooth end into the "ear's" extremity. Once both "ears" are stuffed, the spring unit can be installed.

Blind-stitching a cushion opening. When a cushion cover such as the cover for an ottoman's attached cushion has no zipper, you have to hand-stitch its opening shut after the cover has been stuffed. Follow the technique for blind-stitching given on page 65,

but first pin and stretch the edges to be sewn as explained below.

Place the stuffed cushion face-down on a flat wooden surface at least 2 feet longer than the end of the cushion to be sewn. Fill the cushion's back corners and hollows with loose padding before pinning the opening at the bottom cushion face's edge to the boxing. Push a row of upholsterer's skewers in just behind the cushion face's welt and through the boxing's edge, with the boxing seam allowance turned inside the cushion, to close the opening.

Cut two 18-inch lengths of upholsterer's twine or heavy-duty polyester thread. Form a loose slipknot (see page 100) at one end of each. Drive two tacks partially into the wooden surface, one tack ten inches away from each back cushion corner, in line with the back edge of the cushion. Loop a slipknot over the corner skewer at each back corner; pull the twine taut. Wrap each length of twine around the nearest tack's shank and hammer the tack almost all the way in (see illustration 60).

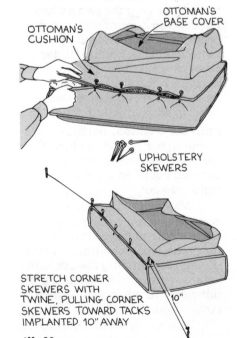

PUSH UPHOLSTERER'S SKEWERS BEHIND WELT AND THROUGH BOXING'S EDGE TO CLOSE ZIPPERLESS CUSHION OPENING

OTTOMAN'S BASE COVER

OTTOMAN'S CUSHION

UPHOLSTERY SKEWERS

STRETCH CORNER SKEWERS WITH TWINE, PULLING CORNER SKEWERS TOWARD TACKS IMPLANTED 10" AWAY

10"

ill. 60

Stretching the cushion's pinned opening like this insures the correct seam alignment and reduces puckering. Now you are ready to begin blind-stitching.

Skirts

Whether your reasons for planning a skirt are purely aesthetic, or also practical—to hide unsightly legs or make your piece look less top-heavy—your furniture will look best if its skirt is well-matched and fitted. Though other skirt styles exist, we recommend a lined, tailored skirt with illusory pleats for fabric economy and construction ease.

Shape, sew, and attach the skirt panels *after* reupholstering your furniture, to insure proper fitting and matching. To do so, you'll need tools for blind-tacking (see page 64) or blind-stitching (see page 65), upholsterer's twine or heavy-duty polyester thread, a ruler, a steam iron, an ironing board or padded surface, and your Measurement List (see pages 40–45).

Skirt-fitting and matching techniques

You will use the same basic techniques to fit the skirt onto your furniture, whether or not your fabric has motifs that require matching (see pages 35–36). The skirt's panel ends will meet at all corners and at each cushion division (if any), where they will be backed by illusory pleat backdrops. If your furniture is to have two or more skirt panels along its front or back, mark the positions of the panel ends on the furniture with T-pins before you begin fitting. Then fit and match the skirt panels to your furniture, using the following directions.

Step 1: Place your furniture on a level surface and mark skirt's top-edge height every six inches with pins.

Step 2: If you're working with fabric that need not be centered or matched, double-check each panel's width at skirt's top-edge height and its length from top-edge height to floor before cutting panels from fabric bolt. Add the necessary nine inches to the width and one inch to the length for allowances. Label each panel's top edge and note where the panel belongs along the circumference of your furniture—for example, a three-deck-cushion sofa's front panels would be labelled front right, front center, and front left.

If you're chalking skirt panels on a fabric with dominant, vertically run motifs or stripes, first consult the centering and matching instructions on pages 35–36. Once you've matched a motif along each skirt panel's length so that the motif will flow evenly up onto the reupholstered furniture's front (many stripes—called "one-way stripes"—must be similarly matched), chalk each panel section's top and bottom edges. Then make each panel section's width equivalent to the fabric bolt's entire width. When you cut out these extra-wide panel sections, you can easily match skirt's motifs or stripes with those on your reupholstered furniture by moving each panel horizontally along the appropriate section of furniture until you find the proper match.

Step 3: Holding a skirt panel against the appropriate furniture section (if your fabric has dominant motifs or stripes, align panel so skirt's motif matches that on furniture above), place pins in panel to mark corners or cushion divisions (if any) which define the two ends of panel's intended finished width. (If your fabric doesn't require matching, these

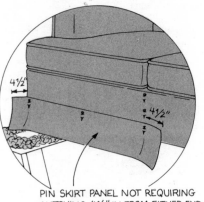

PIN SKIRT PANEL NOT REQUIRING MATCHING 4½" IN FROM EITHER END

ill. 61

pins should be 4½ inches in from either end.) Remove panel; fold, wrong sides together, along panel's length at pinned marks. Press folds flat with steam iron.

If your fabric has dominant motifs or stripes, measure and mark 4½ inches beyond fold at each end of panel, for allowances. Cut off any excess panel width beyond allowance marks. (You'll use excess panel width later—if sufficient—to make pleat backdrops.) Label panel as directed in Step 2.

Step 4: After fitting all panels as in Step 3, cut pleat backdrops (for backdrop dimensions, consult your Measurement List—see pages 40–45).

Step 5: For each skirt panel, cut a lining; dimensions of each lining should be the panel's total length (including allowances) by the panel's width (minus allowances, plus one inch for seams). Cut linings for pleat backdrops the same size as the backdrops themselves. Label all linings as you cut them.

Step 6: On fabric's wrong side, chalk ½-inch seamlines on each skirt panel's and pleat backdrop's bottom edge and ends. On fabric's right side, chalk ½-inch seamlines on each skirt panel's top.

Step 7: Before you sit down to sew, stack panels together; then stack linings in identical order. Place all skirt components, including welt strips, on a flat surface near your sewing machine.

Putting it all together

You can easily make a neat-looking tailored skirt if you take your time and follow your chalked seam lines carefully. The following steps will help you sew both the skirt and its illusory pleat backdrops.

Step 1: Unfold one end of a skirt panel and place panel, right side down, on matching lining section, with panel's end 3½ inches in from lining's end. Align panel's and lining's bottom edges; join panel's end to lining with a ½-inch seam.

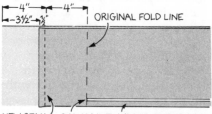

① UNFOLD ONE SKIRT-PANEL END. PLACE ON LINING 3½" FROM LINING'S END

NEW SEAM   CHALK LINE   WRONG SIDE OF SKIRT

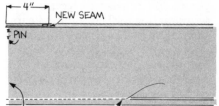

② FOLD SKIRT PANEL BACK OVER NEW SEAM. FOLD AGAIN AT ITS ORIGINAL FOLD

NEW SEAM

PIN

ORIGINAL FOLD   ③ STITCH ALONG CHALK LINE

ill. 62

Step 2: Fold skirt panel back over its new seam, right side up; then fold it again at its original fold mark, right side down, so its original fold mark is aligned with lining's end; pin in place at panel's top.

Step 3: Repeat Steps 1 and 2 to sew skirt panel's other end to lining.

Step 4: With panel still on top, join panel to lining at bottom edge with ½-inch seam along chalk line.

Step 5: Turn panel right side out. Push corners out gently with screwdriver or upholsterer's skewer to make them square.

Step 6: With lining on top, press panel ends and bottom edge seam flat. Bottom seam, when pressed, should lie exactly at lined panel's bottom edge, so no lining shows below panel's outside face.

Step 7: With panel on top, join lining to panel's top with ½-inch seam.

Step 8: Repeat Steps 1 through 7 to sew linings to remaining skirt panels.

Step 9: Place a pleat backdrop, right side down, on matching lining section; align all raw edges. Sew ½-inch seam at ends and bottom edge. Turn backdrop right side out; push corners out gently to make them square. Repeat for remaining backdrops. Press seams flat with lining on top.

Step 10: To make welt casing, join enough welt strips to go around furniture at skirt's top perimeter. Make sure you add eight inches for handling. Wrap welt casing around furniture at skirt height to check for correct length. Remove from furniture; complete welt by sewing as directed on pages 53–54.

Step 11: With a side or back panel on top, stack completed skirt panels in the order in which they'll appear on furniture, to prepare to join them with welt.

Step 12: Letting welt's end extend 4 inches past first panel's end, align welt along ½-inch seam at panel's top, raw edges of seam allowances together. Measure from panel's bottom edge to welt cord to insure correct finished skirt length. Sewing

along welt seam, attach welt to panel's top.

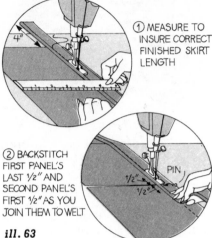

ALIGN WELT ALONG ½" SEAM AT SKIRT PANEL'S TOP

① MEASURE TO INSURE CORRECT FINISHED SKIRT LENGTH

② BACKSTITCH FIRST PANEL'S LAST ½" AND SECOND PANEL'S FIRST ½" AS YOU JOIN THEM TO WELT

PIN

ill. 63

Step 13: Two inches before you reach panel's end, place second panel adjacent to first—ends touching but not overlapping, and bottom edges aligned.

Step 14: Backstitch first panel's last ½ inch and second panel's first ½ inch as you join them with welt. Then continue sewing welt to second panel as in Step 12.

Step 15: Repeat Steps 13 and 14 to join remaining panels with welt, until you are within three inches of last panel's end. Bring skirt's other end around—*making sure panels aren't twisted*—and align the two panel ends as in Step 13, to make a circle. Join welt ends as explained on page 90; finish sewing along welt seam to join panels together.

Step 16: Lining on top, press seam allowances down so welt cord rims finished skirt's top edge.

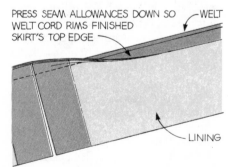

PRESS SEAM ALLOWANCES DOWN SO WELT CORD RIMS FINISHED SKIRT'S TOP EDGE — WELT

LINING

ill. 64

Attaching the skirt

If some or all of your furniture's rails are at the height of your skirt's top edge, blind-tacking your skirt to them saves time. Wherever the rails are not at the appropriate height, you'll need to blind-stitch the skirt to your furniture's new outer cover. Whichever method (or combination of methods) you use, begin as in the following steps.

Step 1: Lifting furniture legs one at a time, slip skirt on from bottom up. Align panel divisions with corners and cushion divisions.

Step 2: Slip-tack skirt's top edge to furniture's corners at correct height wherever skirt can be blind-tacked into position. Wherever it is to be blind-stitched, secure it to outer cover with upholsterer's skewers.

Step 3: Measure and cut a length of upholsterer's twine or heavy-duty polyester thread equal to your furniture's circumference at skirt's top-edge height, plus ten inches. Doubling five inches of twine over at one end,

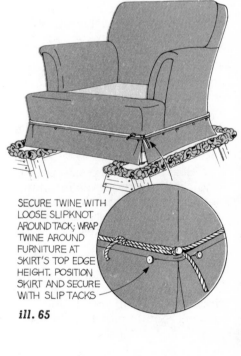

SECURE TWINE WITH LOOSE SLIPKNOT AROUND TACK; WRAP TWINE AROUND FURNITURE AT SKIRT'S TOP EDGE HEIGHT. POSITION SKIRT AND SECURE WITH SLIP TACKS

ill. 65

form a loose slipknot (see page 100). Drive a #10 tack partially in at one front corner of furniture at skirt's top-edge height and loop slipknot over tack. Wrap twine tautly around furniture at skirt's top-edge height; secure twine's other end by looping it around tack.

Step 4: At 6-inch intervals, slip-tack or skewer skirt *immediately* below welt, using twine as your guide for height.

Blind-tacking skirt. Starting at your furniture's front (if the rail height allows for blind-tacking; if not, begin as close to the front as possible), lift the skirt panels and hammer in tacks at 6-inch intervals through the underlying folded seam allowances, until you've tacked all the way around the skirt's circumference (or as far as rails are available).

Remove the slip tacks, then follow the instructions on page 65 for adding a cardboard tacking strip.

To install a pleat backdrop at each corner and cushion division of your furniture, lift the adjacent skirt panels and center the pleat backdrop evenly at the corner or cushion division, under the skirt panels. Slip-tack the backdrop with one tack on each side, one inch from the furniture's corner. The backdrop's bottom edge should align with the bottom edges of the skirt panels. Drive the slip tacks in. Fold the backdrops down at an angle, as shown in illustration 66, to keep

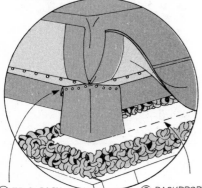

① FOLD BACK-DROP TOPS DOWN AT AN ANGLE TO KEEP SKIRT CORNERS FROM BULGING

② BACKDROP'S BOTTOM EDGE SHOULD ALIGN WITH SKIRT PANELS' BOTTOM EDGES

ill. 66

the skirt corners from bulging. Hammer four tacks in on each side of the furniture's corner.

Blind-stitching skirt. Starting at corner of your furniture nearest area where blind-stitching is necessary, blind-stitch the skirt's top edge to the outer cover, using the method explained on page 65.

Center, skewer, and fold down the pleat backdrops as explained for blind-tacking, above. Blind-stitch the backdrops to the outer cover; remove the skewers.

Upholstery Buttons

Twine-held buttons are often used to break monotony on tight-back furniture. On open-frame padded surfaces, such as inside backs and arms, buttons are secured by twine and installed before any outside covers; solid base surfaces, such as arm posts, however, have buttons tacked or nailed to them after the upholstering is completed. If your old cover sports buttons, measure their positions before removing cover so you'll know where to attach buttons when you put the new cover on.

Make your own twine-held or tack buttons by following the upcoming steps. Or take fabric scraps to an upholsterer who, for a nominal fee, will assemble them for you.

Making twine-held buttons

To make a twine-held button, you need waxed tufting twine, regular sewing needle, dressmaker's weight thread, fabric scraps, dabs of cotton padding, shears, and a button base.

Step 1: Cut a length of upholsterer's twine 30 inches long. Loop it through the two holes in a flat dressmaker's button (available at fabric shops) so that the two strands are the same length.

Step 2: From outer-cover scrap, cut a circle 1½ inches

larger in diameter than the flat button. Double a 20-inch length of dressmaker's thread through a small straight sewing needle; knot the ends together with an overhand knot (see page 100).

Step 3: Take small stitches around the fabric circle ⅛ inch in from the fabric's edge. Leave the needle end of the thread dangling, with the needle in it.

Step 4: Put a bit of cotton padding on the wrong side of the fabric; place the flat button on top of the padding, dangling twine up. Holding the button down with one hand, cinch the fabric around the button by pulling the thread taut. Tie off the thread by making two additional stitches and securing each with an overhand knot.

Here's how to attach finished buttons to your furniture:

Step 1: Using T-pins, mark button positions on your furniture's already-installed inside-back outer cover.

Step 2: Thread both ends of the upholsterer's twine through the eye of a straight 12-inch upholsterer's needle. Let the button hang 6 to 8 inches (inside-back depth) from the needle's eye.

Step 3: Remove a T-pin and push the needle through the hole. From the furniture's rear, reach for the needle and pull it through an outside-back strip of webbing.

Step 4: Remove the needle and pull the twine ends taut. Form a loose upholsterer's slipknot (see page 100). Place a wad of cotton padding between the knot and the webbing, then tighten the knot.

Step 5: After you've attached all the buttons, secure each slipknot with two overhand knots, and snip off excess twine.

Furniture's Insides

If you've concluded that your furniture needs more serious reconditioning than just a fresh layer of cotton padding and a new cover over the burlap, this chapter is for you.

You may only need to reinforce the webbing on coil spring-based furniture, leaving the stuffing underlayers undisturbed, and stripping only the outer covers as directed in Chapter 5. But if you discover bumps or hollows by running your palm across the seat and back, the tops of the springs and perhaps even the bottoms need work. Or if your furniture has acquired a disagreeable odor from smoke, mildew, or a pet, the stuffings must be replaced. Work on springs or stuffings must be preceded by further stripping, to gain access to your furniture's insides.

No matter how many of your furniture's components—arms, back, seat—you have to delve into, strip and reassemble one component completely (including fresh padding and the new outer cover) before tackling the next. This procedure not only eases your reupholstering task by keeping loosened interior stuffings out of your way, but also enables you to see how each cover section is fitted to the furniture. Because of the way cover sections and their stretchers connect, repair components in this order: first, the deck or tight seat; next, the inside arms, then the inside wings (if present), and, following that, the inside back. Finish up with the outside wings (if present), then the outside arms, and last, the outside back.

No doubt your own piece of furniture differs from the armchair that stars in this book. But you will more easily avoid mistakes in dismantling your own piece if you follow the steps used to dismantle the chair shown here.

Step by step: Stripping a fully upholstered armchair in order to reach springs and frame

1 Place chair upright.

2 Using two tacks on each stretcher, slip-tack (hammer tacks in only partially) any arm and back stretchers to wood arm and back liners. (See illustration 1 detailing parts of chair frame.)

Tacks hold stretchers out of the way while you're working on deck.

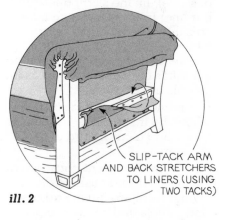

SLIP-TACK ARM AND BACK STRETCHERS TO LINERS (USING TWO TACKS)

ill. 2

3 Lift front of lip to seam where it joins decking; remove cotton padding from under lip.

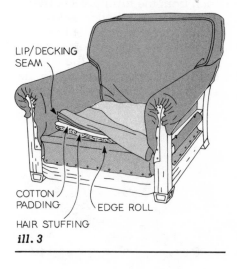

LIP/DECKING SEAM

COTTON PADDING

EDGE ROLL

HAIR STUFFING

ill. 3

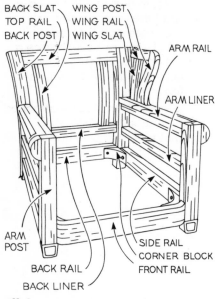

BACK SLAT
TOP RAIL
BACK POST
WING POST
WING RAIL
WING SLAT
ARM RAIL
ARM LINER
ARM POST
SIDE RAIL
CORNER BLOCK
FRONT RAIL
BACK RAIL
BACK LINER

ill. 1

4 Snip twine that moors lip/decking seam to underlying muslin or burlap.

5 While pushing springs down around the edges to release fabric and stuffing, remove as a unit the outer-cover lip and decking, cotton padding, and any hair or other stuffing beneath it. Set aside outer cover as visual aid for installing the new one. If they're in good condition, save padding and hair layers, as a unit, for reuse.

6 Snip any twine that holds loose or rubberized hair on top of lip's edge roll. If it's in good condition, save hair for reuse in same shape as molded.

7 Snip twine that moors edge roll to burlap and to edgewire beneath. If it's in good condition, save edge roll for reuse.

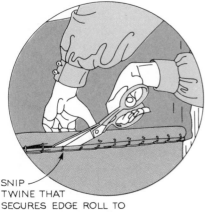

SNIP TWINE THAT SECURES EDGE ROLL TO BURLAP AND EDGE WIRE

ill. 4

8 Remove tacks securing muslin undercover, if any, and discard both muslin and tacks.

9 Snip any twine that moors cotton padding and hair to the burlap covering the springs. Remove padding and hair as a unit; if they're in good condition, save them for reuse.

10 Remove any hair and/or cotton padding wedged between arm liner and side rail on each side of chair. If it's in good condition, save it for reuse in same shape as molded.

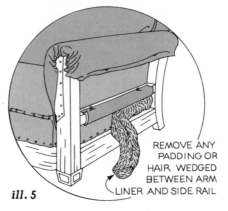

REMOVE ANY PADDING OR HAIR WEDGED BETWEEN ARM LINER AND SIDE RAIL

ill. 5

11 Remove tacks from burlap at front, back, and side rails. Sever any twine that moors burlap to edgewire and to springs. Lift burlap from spring tops; save for future use, if in good condition.

REMOVE TACKS FROM BURLAP ALONG RAILS

ill. 6

12 To dismantle inside back, follow procedures similar to those in Steps 1, 2, 5 (removing inside back's outer cover and stuffing), 8, 9, and 11. Don't throw anything away (except muslin undercover, if there is one) unless you are certain it cannot be reused.

Arms ordinarily contain no springs; usually you need to strip arms only in order to smooth out or replace their stuffing. (Stuffings are discussed on pages 109–110.)

Webbing

The following guidelines will help you to reinforce sagging webbing

and resecure coil spring bottoms to that webbing. Sometimes spring bottoms are held fast to the webbing by upholsterer's twine, and sometimes by hog rings (heavy staples pinched into loops). Spring bottoms held by hog rings usually stay in position even if you reinforce the old webbing with new. Spring bottoms moored with twine, however, may need to be resecured.

Check the old twine thoroughly. If you spy loose twine ends, or you find the bottom-coil twine seems slack when plucked, or the spring bottoms seem to move when you feel them through the webbing, plan on remooring the spring bottoms (see page 100) after you've renewed the webbing.

If you're working with a deck that rests on coil springs, there are good arguments for tacking new webbing over the old rather than taking the old webbing off. This shortcut saves time, increases the thickness of the springs' foundation, and best of all, saves you the effort of building the seat base from scratch. If you remove the old webbing, you not only have to reweb the entire frame base, but also position the springs correctly, re-anchor them to the webbing, and retie their tops for proper support. Even if the webbing is somewhat damaged, you will do better to reinforce it rather than remove it.

The argument changes if no springs exist (as in pad seats—see page 79) or if the coil springs are anchored to burlap rather than webbing (as is sometimes the case in backs). In such situations, removing the old webbing or burlap neither takes as much time nor jeopardizes the mooring of any springs. And in these cases, by replacing old webbing with new, you minimize the chances of unsightly lumps disfiguring the new cover's appearance.

Basic rewebbing techniques.
Securing webbing to wood constitutes one of upholstering's simpler skills. For most webbing tasks, you need a stretcher tool (used to pull strips taut) in addition to tacks and a hammer. Several models of stretcher tools exist. Your main concern in selecting one is to insure that neither the stretcher nor the webbing will slip when you pull each strip taut.

Traditional webbing tacks are double-barbed. These, however, are difficult to find and difficult to pry free, should you err in placing them. For most woods, #12 tacks work fine; however, #8 tacks should be used for antiques. When in doubt about the proper size, remove a tack from the existing webbing; choose a size larger if you'll be rewebbing on top of the old layer.

Whether you are reinforcing old webbing beneath a sofa, or applying new webbing to a pad-seated chair's bare frame, affix each strip as directed in the following steps. Before you begin, chalk the positions of the new strips on the rails to prevent misalignment. On a coil spring-based seat or back, place each webbing strip at the center of a row of springs in order to give the springs maximum support.

Step 1: Turn chair upside-down.

Step 2: Position webbing roll's free end one inch past wood frame's outer edge.

Step 3. Hammer in four tacks, evenly spaced apart, roughly in a line ½ inch from frame's outer edge, but slightly staggered to prevent the wood from splitting. (The ½-inch setback leaves enough frame bare for you to attach outer cover later.) If a new

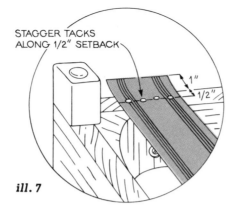

ill. 7

tack slips into an old hole, or a new point blunts on an old tack head, remove and start again. This happens less frequently than you may fear.

Step 4: Fold webbing's free end back over the four tacks. Flat-

ill. 8

ten fold with hammer and secure with three more tacks, slightly staggered.

Step 5: Pull webbing to opposite side of furniture frame, letting roll rest on table or ground. Don't cut webbing before stretching and tacking.

Step 6: Place hammer and seven tacks within easy reach.

Step 7: Pull webbing taut. Placing stretcher tool's cushioned end against outer side of frame at a 45° angle, wrap webbing over stretcher tool's spiked end.

Step 8: With webbing gripped securely, pull down on stretcher tool (the furniture's frame is your fulcrum) until maximum tension is reached and you fear that further pulling may snap frame.

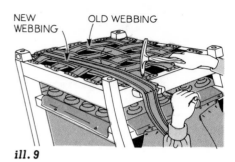

ill. 9

Step 9: With your free hand, test webbing's tautness by bouncing a tack hammer's head on it—the webbing should produce a lively rebound of the hammer. Repeat Steps 7–8 to tighten the webbing even more if your first efforts didn't pass the test.

Step 10: Hold stretcher tool steady so that webbing stays taut. Hammer in first tack ½ inch from frame's outer edge, near webbing border. Place second tack ½ inch from frame's edge at webbing's opposite border; space the next two evenly in between. Stagger the four tacks slightly to prevent the wood from splitting and loosening webbing.

Step 11: Release stretcher tool; sever webbing from roll one inch beyond frame's outer edge.

Step 12: Fold webbing's end back over the four tacks, flattening fold with hammer and securing it with three more tacks, slightly staggered.

Step by step: Reinforcing the webbing of a fully upholstered armchair's deck

If you heed the following suggestions, you probably won't need to remove the old webbing, no matter what type of coil-spring-based furniture you're working on.

1 Hammer old webbing tacks down tight.

2 Using the techniques given in Steps 1–12 on page 98, place first strip of new webbing near front rail's midsection, running front to back. Even though old webbing may not be centered under a spring row, make sure new webbing is before tacking.

3 Center each new webbing strip over a spring row (not necessarily over each strip of old webbing), until you have completed front-to-back rows.

4 Place first strip of cross webbing near side rail's midsection, running to opposite side rail. For added strength, interweave new cross webbing with new front-to-back webbing.

5 Interweave and center a new cross webbing strip over each side-to-side spring row, using the techniques given in Steps 1–12 on page 98. Save front row of springs for last.

6 If front row of springs is placed very close to front rail, you may have to cut a corner out of last cross webbing strip at each end, in order to center webbing over springs and fit it around front legs.

First, holding free end of webbing strip in position—

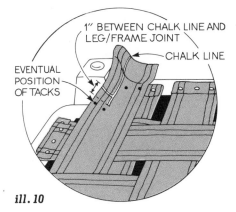

ill. 10

centered over spring row and against chair leg—chalk T-shaped cutting line on webbing, with the T's cross bar running from strip's free end to leg's inner edge (the edge perpendicular to webbing), and the T's vertical bar joining its cross bar at a perpendicular angle, one inch from leg/front rail joint, as in illustration 10. Cut along chalk line. Secure resulting long strip of free end to side rail with two tacks; fold end over and tack again. Secure short strip of free end with two tacks on bottom of front rail, just shy of the leg/rail joint. Fold end over and tack again.

Now stretch this webbing strip as you did all the others (it won't lie flat near leg at opposite side), but hammer only two tacks to opposite side rail across half its width before severing it from roll. Make a 2-inch cut along strip, dividing strip width in two; fold end of tacked half over and secure to side rail with another two tacks. Pull free half taut with hand; secure to front rail with two tacks, just shy of leg/front rail joint. Snip

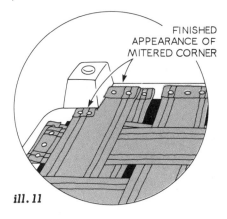

ill. 11

strip one inch past tacks. Fold end back and secure with two more tacks to front rail.

Webbing variations for furniture parts other than decks. You can use webbing for furniture constructions other than coil spring-based decks. Install webbing in backs and arms with caution to determine the amount of stretcher-tool pressure they can tolerate—some are frail. Don't worry if you can't pull arm and back webbing as taut as seat webbing; these components aren't subject to as much pressure as a person's weight exerts on a seat. For sag seats and sag backs, you won't need a stretcher tool.

Some typical webbing patterns are shown here, though your best guide is your furniture's old webbing. Note that spring-based decks and backs are webbed on the outside surfaces of their frames, whereas springless decks, backs, and arms are webbed on the inside surfaces of their frames.

ill. 12

Spring supports other than webbing. The most common alternatives to webbing used to support coil springs are wire or perforated metal bands. If either has come loose from the frame, but the metal remains sound, replace the old tacks or screws with new ones.

Often a wire support (less frequently, a metal band) will have snapped or rusted through. Reinforcing it with webbing may prove simpler than trying to fashion or purchase metal reinforcements. If you're dealing with broken wire, cut or file free its links to the frame as close to the springs as possible. Remove wire remnants and any attendant tacks, then replace them with webbing, following the steps on page 98.

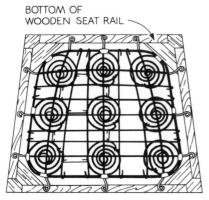

BOTTOM OF
WOODEN SEAT RAIL

CUT AND REMOVE ALL COLORED PORTIONS
OF WIRE AND REPLACE WITH TWINE—
CAUTION: DO NOT CUT SPRING EDGE SUPPORT

ill. 13

If you're dealing with damaged metal bands, simply install webbing over them.

You may discover that wood slats or a plywood sheet supports your springs. Leave slats alone; replace plywood with webbing to give the furniture a more cushioned feeling.

Resewing coil-spring bottoms firmly to webbing. If hog rings anchor the bottoms of your piece's springs firmly to the old webbing, you needn't resecure the bottoms. However, springs that are moored to the webbing with twine, and springs hog-ringed to burlap need cinching up if the

springs can be shifted against their webbing or burlap base.

To begin the cinching process, thread a straight 12 to 18-inch upholsterer's needle (a double-pointed straight needle—if you can get one—makes the task even easier) with upholsterer's twine or heavy-duty polyester thread. Mooring each spring's bottom coil at three evenly-spaced points to the webbing or burlap keeps the coil where it belongs. Work from the top side of the frame so that you can see the location of the springs, and be careful not to move the springs out of position while sewing.

As you anchor the spring bottoms to the webbing, you'll employ two types of knots: the "upholsterer's slipknot" (illustration 14) when you start sewing, and the "overhand knot" (illustration 15) when you finish.

THE UPHOLSTERER'S SLIPKNOT

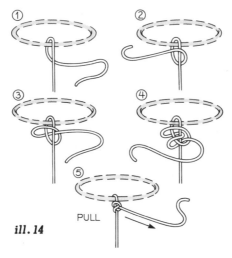

PULL

ill. 14

THE OVERHAND KNOT

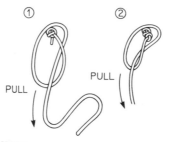

PULL   PULL

ill. 15

Even if your furniture differs from the armchair featured, you can ease your spring-bottom resewing chores by inspecting the drawings and following the steps given below.

Step by step: Resewing coil-spring bottoms to webbing in a fully upholstered armchair's deck

Before you start resewing, place chair upright at a comfortable height on horses or any two supports—you need a clear space in which to pull your needle up and down through the webbing under the chair.

1 Thread needle with as long a length of twine or thread as you can sew with comfortably.

2 Beginning at a corner under chair, push needle up through webbing close to a spring's bottom coil and down on the other side of coil's wire, forming a loop over the wire. This constitutes your first stitch. Pull twine through webbing so that about an eight-inch length is left hanging at starting point.

3 Tie upholsterer's slipknot as shown in illustration 14. Hold long end of twine steady while pulling short end so that knot is pulled up against webbing. Secure slipknot with two overhand knots as shown.

4 Bringing twine across coil, push needle up through webbing at another point about ⅓ of the way around coil's inner edge. As in Step 2, catch bottom coil in a stitch as you push needle down through webbing.

5 Planning your stitches according to illustration 16, so that the third stitch on each coil is positioned closest to edge of next

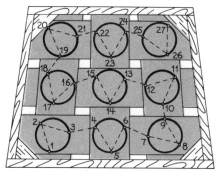

STITCHING PATTERN FOR COIL SPRINGS, AS SEEN FROM ABOVE. DOTTED LINES SHOW PATTERN TWINE MAKES ON UNDERSIDE OF WEBBING

ill. 16

spring, stitch coil down at third and last point, another ⅓ of the way around coil, and nearest to an adjacent spring.

6 Move to next coil. Mooring each coil in three places, follow the dots signifying stitches on the diagram until you're about to run out of twine.

7 Lock last stitch by looping twine from previous stitch around needle twice as it emerges through webbing, then tightening twine with a quick jerk. Secure twine end with two half hitches placed close to the webbing.

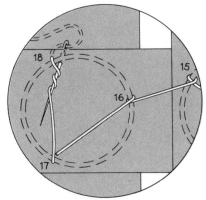

AS VIEWED FROM BOTTOM OF CHAIR: PULL NEEDLE THROUGH LOOPS AND PULL TAUT

ill. 17

8 Begin each new length of twine by following Steps 1 through 3. End each length of twine by looping it around needle twice, and securing with two half hitches, as in Step 7.

9 When all spring bottoms are resewn, and last twine length is knotted off, trim any dangling twine ends to one inch.

Springs

Even if your springs need work, you're still in luck: furniture with springs is more comfortable than furniture without. Once privy to some tricks the professionals use, you'll call your own springing labors a snap.

Meet three springs. Coils—the most sought-after of springs—boast hourglass figures and a reputation for providing maximum comfort. Zigzags, though easy to yoke to each other, balk when asked to stretch themselves out for refastening to the frame.

Because coils are more traditional than zigzags, you may be tempted to switch from one to the other during the reupholstering process. Don't do it. Your frame's dimensions and its strength were probably reckoned by the springs it now holds.

Less prevalent than coils or zigzags are the rubber-strap springs (also called "rubber webbing") that sometimes appear on Scandinavian imports. You can easily attach rubber replacement straps by stretching them with your hands and tacking them in position as though they were webbing (see pages 98–99 for information on tacking webbing).

Common spring problems. Problems with loose coil-spring bottoms are discussed on page 100. If your coil springs remain sound and firmly fixed to the webbing but their tops have worked loose from each other, retie their tops as described on pages 102–105. To insure a smooth surface on which to layer stuffing, you'll want to retie all the springs even if only one is out of line.

If an unruly zigzag spring is troubling you, batten it down by

hammering existing or new nails into the frame through the metal clips designed to hold it in place. If a clip is broken, replace it with another purchased from an upholstery shop.

Once in a while you'll discover that the metal in a coil-spring has snapped. You'll have to remove the broken spring completely and replace it, following the two steps below. Springs are sold in many lengths and gauges (heavier for seats, lighter for backs), so take your broken spring with you to help your upholstery wholesaler or professional upholsterer supply its duplicate.

Step 1: Cut only the twine linking broken spring's top coil to its neighbors or to edgewire. Leave severed ends of twine alone, and keep rest of twine tied so as not to loosen more springs. If broken coil is attached to edgewire with clip, pry clip open and save.

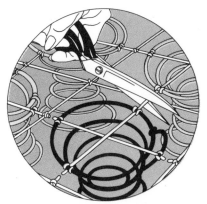

CUT TWINE LINKING BROKEN SPRING'S TOP COIL TO ITS NEIGHBORS

ill. 18

Step 2: Cut twine that joins broken spring's bottom coil to webbing. (If hog rings are used instead of twine, remove them. When reanchoring spring later, use twine.) Pull twine ends up at nearest stitches on adjacent springs, then secure ends to adjacent springs' bottom coils with two half hitches each.

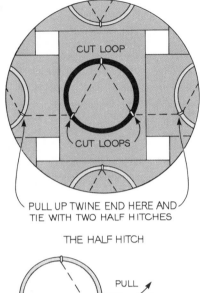

LOOKING DOWN ON BOTTOM COIL OF SPRING
(BROKEN SPRING IN CENTER)

CUT LOOP

CUT LOOPS

PULL UP TWINE END HERE AND TIE WITH TWO HALF HITCHES

THE HALF HITCH

PULL

ill. 19

Position new spring in exact spot from which you removed old spring. If you removed an edgewire clip in Step 1, reuse it to clamp top coil of new spring to edgewire.

Using stitching technique on page 100, attach new spring to webbing, starting first new stitch on nearest point of an adjacent spring, where you secured twine end with half hitches. Move to new spring, mooring its bottom coil in three equidistant stitches. If you secured twine ends on a second adjacent spring, stitch that spot, too, before knotting off new twine as indicated on page 101.

Retie new spring's top along with other springs, as described on page 97.

Basic retying techniques. Rather than search for fancier fastenings when the time comes to retie your springs, you can link either zigzag springs or coil-spring tops into position with a heavy-duty twine known as "spring twine"—6 ply, #60 works fine. When you need to

secure the spring twine to the frame, use a twin-tack cloverleaf (see illustration below). To form a twin-tack cloverleaf, center and slip-tack two tacks (#8 for hardwoods, #12 for softer woods), ½ inch apart, at the end of each row of springs, on top of the back, front, and side rails.

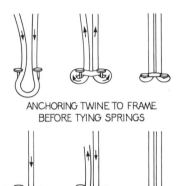

TWIN-TACK CLOVERLEAF

ANCHORING TWINE TO FRAME BEFORE TYING SPRINGS

SECURING TWINE AFTER TYING SPRINGS
ill. 20

Loop one end of each length of spring twine you expect to use to tie a row of springs (directions follow), leaving 15 inches of it free to form the short end. Slip the loop between the tacks with the loose ends dangling inside the frame, then fold the loop over as shown in illustration 20. Pull the twine ends taut before you hammer the tacks in, locking the twin-tack cloverleaf in place. Secure the spring twine after tying the springs by forming another twin-tack cloverleaf on the opposite rail.

To yoke each zag, zig, or coil to another with spring twine, tie a clove hitch (see illustration 21).

THE CLOVE HITCH

① ②

③ ④

ill. 21

Should the twine break, the clove hitches will prevent all the knots from loosening in a chain reaction.

As you tie springs together with new twine, leave the old twine or other fasteners undisturbed wherever possible. These old links not only guide your current efforts but thicken the 'net' that keeps burlap from sagging, and stuffing from dropping through into the springs.

Step by step: Retying all coil-spring tops in a fully upholstered armchair's spring-edge deck

The techniques given here for retying the tops of a set of coil springs apply to both spring-edge decks and backs, and are useful no matter what type of furniture you're reupholstering. Variations to suit flat and rounded hard-edge seats and backs, barrel-backs, and furniture with zigzag springs appear on page 105.

1 Make sure perimeter springs' top coils are held fast to edgewire wherever they touch it. If metal clips are used at edgewire, tighten them with pliers, if necessary. If an edgewire clip or twine has snapped, remove remaining twine or parts of clip. Resecure coil to edgewire with a yard of upholsterer's twine or heavy-duty polyester thread, using a knot called "lysco lash" (see illustration 22).

THE LYSCO LASH

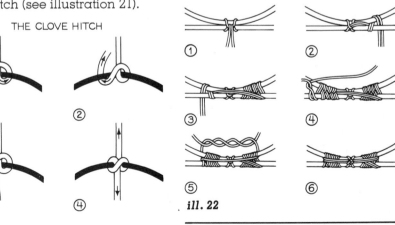

① ②

③ ④

⑤ ⑥

ill. 22

2 Check to see that the inside top edge of the frame's front rail is rounded. If not, bevel it with hammerhead's side or file it down with a wood rasp; a sharp frame edge wears down twines securing springs to front rail.

3 Measure distance from back rail's outer edge to outer edge of front rail; triple this measurement to determine correct twine length. Cut a length of spring twine for every back-to-front row of springs.

4 On back and front rails, at the approximate center of each spring row (adjacent to old tacks), slip-tack two tacks, ½ inch apart. Anchor each twine length to a set of tacks on back rail (point A in illustration 23), following the twin-tack cloverleaf method shown in illustration 20. Be sure to leave about 15 inches free for the short end of twine. You'll use the short end to adjust back springs' height after tying other springs with the long end.

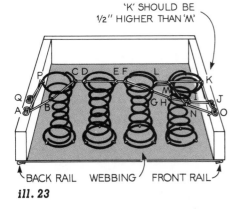

'K' SHOULD BE ½" HIGHER THAN 'M'

BACK RAIL   WEBBING   FRONT RAIL

ill. 23

5 Starting at a spring row not adjacent to side rails, loop twine over third coil of back spring (point B in illustration 23). Push spring toward rail while you pull twine taut. Hold twine loop tautly in place with one hand and form a clove hitch (see illustration

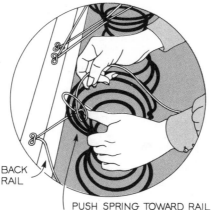

BACK RAIL

PUSH SPRING TOWARD RAIL WHILE FORMING CLOVE HITCH

ill. 24

on page 102) with the other, knotting the loop in place. When knot is secure, spring should lean slightly towards rail.

6 Attach another clove hitch to opposite side of same spring's top coil (point C in illustration 23). Twine should extend tautly from knot at point B to knot at point C.

7 Push neighboring spring top in back-to-front row toward spring you just tied. Catch its top coil with a clove hitch at spot nearest spring you just tied (point D in illustration 23). Make sure twine is taut between the two springs. When knot is secure, both springs should stand straight up and down and be at the same height. If not, you should readjust the last knot. To do so, loosen clove hitch by pushing spring tops together and undoing knot with the help of an upholsterer's skewer. Adjust springs to proper position and resecure knot so twine is taut.

8 Catch same spring with a second clove hitch on opposite side of top coil (point E in 23), extending twine tautly between point D and point E.

9 Repeat Step 7 on third spring in back-to-front row (point F in illustration 23). From this point on through points G, H, I, and J, you'll gradually slope twine down towards front rail. This method of

tying spring tops reduces the crown at the middle of a flat seat and strengthens the perimeter springs.

10 Repeat Step 8 on third spring, but attach the clove hitch to second coil down, on opposite side of spring (point G in illustration 23).

11 Before you tie next spring (the one nearest front rail), check to see if old twine holds it at proper height (between 3 and 4 inches above top of front rail). If you want to reduce the height of this front spring, push third spring down as you attach twine to third coil down on front spring (point H in illustration 23). If you do not have to adjust height of spring, simply push front spring's top toward the one behind it when you knot its third coil at point H.

12 Catch same spring with a clove hitch on opposite side (point I in illustration 23), as in Step 8.

13 Now loop twine around one of the two slip tacks aligned on front rail with the row of springs you're tying (point J in illustration 23). Pull twine until the three back springs are at the right height and in upright position. The third coil of the front spring may lean towards rail slightly to accomplish this. Drive tack in.

14 Loop twine around second slip tack aligned with row of springs, forming a twin-tack cloverleaf (see illustration 20), and hammer tack in. Leave remaining twine hanging.

15 Repeat Steps 4 through 14 on remaining back-to-front rows.

16 Starting with spring nearest front rail in center back-to-front row, loop remaining twine over top coil's outer edge (attached to edgewire). Push spring down so that front edge of top coil is ½ inch above height established by rear springs, and secure spring with clove hitch at point K in illustration 23. Before tightening knot, measure from front rail up to spring top to insure that the spring is at correct height for tying. This is especially important if old twine holding spring's outer edge has snapped.

17 Extend twine over front spring's top coil to top coil of spring behind it, and loop twine around nearest point on that coil (point L in illustration 23). Pull free end of looped twine back toward outer edge of front top coil (point K in illustration 23), then down to the rail. Twine should stretch over top of front coil and make a 90° angle as it bends down to touch outer edge of rail. By pulling, you bring front spring's top coil back slightly toward the one behind it. Now grasp and pinch twine firmly against coil at point M with one hand so that twine won't slip. With the other hand, tie a clove hitch at point M, catching coil and twine leading from point K to point L in the knot.

18 Adjacent to knot made previously at point I, loop remaining twine around front spring's third coil down (point N). Pull twine taut until inner edge of top coil (at point M) is at same height as points C, D, E, F, and L. Secure with a clove hitch.

19 Anchor twine on front rail (point O in illustration 25) in another twin-tack cloverleaf (see page 102). To protect twine from excessive wear where it may chafe against rail's inner edge, wrap

remaining length of twine around the two twine lengths running from spring's third coil to rail. Secure free end with a half hitch.

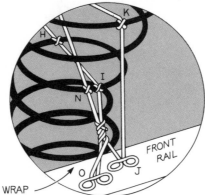

WRAP EXCESS TWINE AND SECURE WITH CLOVE HITCH
ill. 25

20 Repeat steps 16 through 19 on all springs nearest front rail.

21 Starting with spring nearest back rail in center back-to-front row, loop remaining short end of twine over outer edge of top coil (point P in illustration 23). Pull twine taut until point P is at same height as points C, D, E, F, L, and M. Anchor twine on top of back rail to two new tacks, slip-tacked at point Q (in illustration 23), using a twin-tack cloverleaf (see page 102). Drive tacks in. Don't trim off extra twine; you may need it later for spring height adjustment.

22 Repeat step 21 for all springs nearest back rail. This completes your back-to-front spring-top tying.

23 Measure distance from one side rail's outer edge to outer edge of opposite side rail. Double this measurement to determine correct twine length. Cut as many spring twine lengths as there are side-to-side rows of springs.

24 Beginning with a center side-to-side row of springs, tie top of first spring (that closest to a side rail) as you initially tied first spring in each back-to-front row (Steps 4–6, points A–C in illustra-

tion 23). Tie tops of springs between first and last springs as you tied top of second spring in each back-to-front row (Steps 7–8, points D–E). To tie last spring in row (that nearest opposite side rail), reverse Steps 4–6, finishing with twin-tack cloverleaf on top of side rail.

25 Except for slight upward tilt (½ inch) at front rail, spring tops should now form a level surface. To raise or level one or more spring tops, try to pull up or bend top coil of each until level with neighboring springs. If coil won't respond to pulling or bending, you must free twine by loosening tacks, untying all knots in one whole row of springs, and retying row according to instructions above. You may have to release and retie both side-to-side and back-to-front rows in which uneven spring or springs appear.

If one or two springs protrude unevenly, lower them by clove-hitching a length of twine diagonally across their tops and securing it with a twin-tack cloverleaf to each adjacent rail (see illustration 26). If a whole row of springs protrudes, lower it by running another length of twine parallel to your first set of knots (Steps 3–21) but pulling it tighter

USE LENGTH OF TWINE DIAGONALLY TO ADJUST HEIGHT OF ONE OR TWO SPRINGS

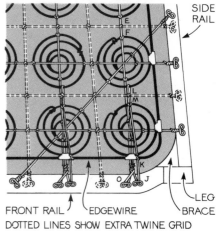

SIDE RAIL
FRONT RAIL EDGEWIRE LEG BRACE
DOTTED LINES SHOW EXTRA TWINE GRID
ill. 26

before anchoring it on back and front rails. When springs are arranged to your satisfaction, and all twine is secured, trim off any extra twine to one inch.

26 Additional twine lengths cross spaces between spring rows in most older furniture, either diagonal to or parallel with the rails. Leave these lengths alone. They not only minimize spring wobble, but help support burlap when you sit.

If no such lengths grace your chair, create them by duplicating with twine the grid of dotted lines in illustration 26. Loop one twine length around another (clove hitches are unnecessary) at every twine intersection both on grid and at new twine linking spring tops. As you pull additional twine taut, take care not to bend springs away from their upright positions. Use twin-tack cloverleafs (see Step 4) to anchor additional twine to rails.

Spring-tying variations. Though furniture comes in almost as great a variety as people, spring-tying variations remain few. If one of these variations applies to your furniture, be sure to read through the previous pages on basic spring tying before you begin to work with the following instructions.

● **Hard-edge coil spring-based seats and backs.** "Hard edge" simply means that the furniture has no edgewire. Most backs are hard edge; hard-edge seats are simpler to retie but sometimes stiffer to sit on than seats boasting edgewire.

To retie a hard-edge seat or back, you'll need lengths of spring twine twice as long as the length or the width of the frame. Even if only one old spring needs replacing or one old twine length has snapped, cut enough new

lengths so that you can retie all the springs, to insure a smooth surface.

Your hard-edge seat or back may be flat or rounded. If it's flat, retie as shown in illustration 27. If it's rounded, tie it as though it were flat except that the twine leading from the twin-tack cloverleaf should be attached to the *top* coil of the spring nearest the frame, not the third coil down.

SPRINGS TIED FOR HARD-EDGE FLAT SEAT

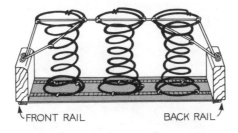

← FRONT RAIL   BACK RAIL →

SPRINGS TIED FOR HARD-EDGE ROUND SEAT

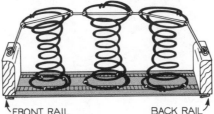

← FRONT RAIL   BACK RAIL →

ill. 27

● **Zigzag seats and backs.** Metal clips fasten the ends of zigzag springs to the frame. These springs must also be linked from side to side, both to the frame and to each other, in order to keep the proper resilience. Usually you'll find hooks or small metal springs doing the job. Sometimes you'll find neither; in that case, you need to add spring twine.

Plan to link zigzags every four to six inches from back to front, and make each single twine length cross the entire frame from side to side. Use the standard twin-tack cloverleaf to anchor the twine to the frame, and clove-hitch it securely to the springs' zigs and zags. Keep twine taut by pulling springs toward each other as you tie, or toward the frame. Take care that each hitch centers at the apex of each zig or zag until

you anchor twine's opposite end, or else the twine may slip.

WOODEN SEAT RAIL

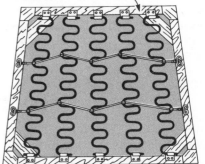

ZIGZAG SPRINGS CAN BE SECURED CROSSWISE BY TWINE LENGTHS KNOTTED TO ZIGZAGS WITH CLOVE HITCHES
ill. 28

● **Coil-spring barrelbacks.** Because the top coils of the springs in most barrel-shaped backs sit closer together than the bottom coils, tie them in a vertical direction—bottom to top—only. If they were tied horizontally, the twine would tend to pull the springs out of alignment (the top coils would strain to move further apart) whenever you lean against the back. For greater stability, run two parallel ties along each row of springs, aligning the twine lengths just off center, ½ inch apart.

STRIPS OF BURLAP TACKED OVER SPRINGS   IN BARREL-SHAPED BACKS, TIE COIL SPRINGS VERTICALLY, USING TWO PARALLEL TIES

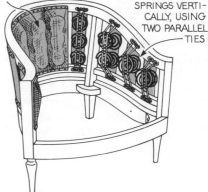

ill. 29

Burlap and edge rolls

Think of an open-face sandwich—a base of burlap piled with stuffings enclosed by an edge roll—to visualize how these interior trimmings are assembled. Their purpose, of course, differs: you lean against or sit on them, rather than wolf them down.

Your furniture may sport more or fewer interior trimmings than it needs. As you reupholster, watch for places where burlap could be added to stop cotton from sagging, or where horse or hog hair could be eliminated to slim a bulgy back.

ELIMINATING SOME OF THE ORIGINAL HAIR SLIMS A BULGY BACK

ill. 30

If you have opened your furniture's insides to work on its springs, you can probably reuse whatever stuffing and edge rolls were originally there. Perhaps you can even reuse some of the original burlap, if its threads aren't rotted with age.

Burlap. Burlap—a loose-woven jute fabric—plays two roles: it keeps stuffing from poking through into the springs or out through the webbing, and it provides a surface on which the stuffing (or padding) can be evenly spread. You use burlap to seal off openings created by the furniture's frame.

Normally all openings except the seat are sealed with burlap on both sides of the frame, to protect the stuffing on the inside arms, inside back, and inside wings, and to cushion the outer cover against unintentional pokes. You also tack burlap over the webbing on springless seats and backs. If the furniture has coil springs, you cover their tops with burlap, and tack it to the frame.

TACK BURLAP OVER WEBBING ON SPRINGLESS BACK

ill. 31

Most fabric shops sell the heavy-duty burlap that you need. Sometimes a friendly professional upholsterer will sell you excess stock.

To determine the proper burlap section size, measure the outside perimeter of the frame around the opening to be sealed and add a 2-inch tacking allowance all the way around. Burlap frays easily; the allowance permits you to fold the burlap in order to tack it through two layers.

Once you've cut the section, smooth it over the opening, and slip-tack it to the frame at the center and end of each side, using # 3 tacks. Where there are obstructions—such as arm posts, arm rails, or back posts—cut burlap as shown in illustration 32.

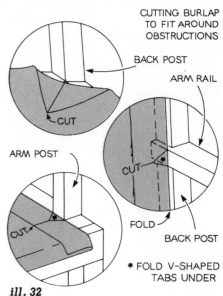

CUTTING BURLAP TO FIT AROUND OBSTRUCTIONS

BACK POST

ARM RAIL

CUT

ARM POST

CUT

FOLD

BACK POST

CUT

* FOLD V-SHAPED TABS UNDER

ill. 32

Step by step: Securing burlap over coil springs of a fully upholstered armchair's spring-edge deck

The following techniques, used to secure burlap over the deck springs of a fully upholstered armchair, work equally well for sprung backs.

1 From outside top of left rail, across springs to outside top of right rail, measure deck's width. Do not depress springs while measuring. Add 4 inches.

2 From outside top of back rail, across springs to outside top of front rail, measure deck's length. Again, do not depress springs. Add 4 inches. This measurement, combined with that from Step 1, determines size of burlap section.

3 On flat surface, measure and cut out burlap section.

4 Center section over springs.

5 Pulling burlap taut without depressing springs, slip-tack it, two inches in from burlap's edges, to top of front rail near rail's outer edge, and center tops of back and sides rails.

6 Still two inches in from burlap's edges, hammer slip-tacks and additional tacks in, 1½ inches apart, on back rail's top. Start at center, working toward each corner. Stagger tacks slightly to keep from splitting wood.

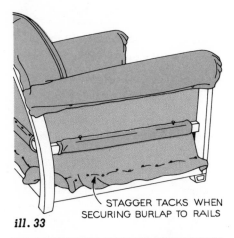

STAGGER TACKS WHEN SECURING BURLAP TO RAILS

ill. 33

7 Cut burlap at arm and back posts, as shown in illustration 32. Fold flaps to fit around back posts and finish tacking burlap near corners of back rail.

8 Taking care to keep burlap taut without depressing springs, tack it to front rail's top.

Start tacking at center, working toward each corner. Three inches from corner, form pleats as shown in illustration 34. Tack pleats down and trim off pleat excess to within ½ inch of tacks.

FORM PLEATS 3″ FROM CORNERS— SECURE WITH TACKS

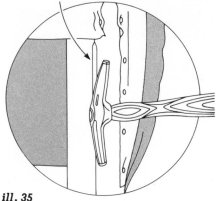

BURLAP CUT TO FIT AROUND ARM POST
ill. 34

9 Tack burlap to tops of side rails. When you get to the corners, fold flaps to fit around arm and back posts, and finish tacking.

10 Fold the 2-inch tacking allowances back over tacks; tack them down, staggering the tacks slightly so as not to split the wood.

Edge rolls. Edge rolls—½-inch to 1½-inch burlap-wrapped cores of paper, rope, hair, or cotton— serve upholstered furniture in several ways. They soften sharp edges, improving comfort and lessening chances that the fabric will fray. They help to contain stuffing. And an edge roll under the furniture's lip hoists a loose cushion's front just enough to keep it from scooting forward when you sit.

You may wonder why you don't soften all edges with edge rolls. There are two reasons: first, if edge rolls are used, you will need extra stuffing or cotton padding to build surfaces level with the rolls' tops, and the more supplies needed, the greater the expense. The second reason is an aesthetic one: a piece of furniture stuffed to bursting pleases no one. If there is a spot where you don't wish to have a stuffed look, but where the fabric is pulled over a sharp edge of the frame, pound the edge into a bevel with your hammerhead's side. By rounding the edge, you will prevent it from chafing your fabric.

BEVEL SHARP EDGES OF WOODEN CHAIR FRAME BY STRIKING WITH SIDE OF HAMMER

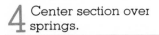

ill. 35

Your furniture displays one of two edge-roll types: ready-made (with a cylindrical cross section) or handmade (with a less cylindrical cross section). Unless the original edge rolls have ripped open or acquired a disagreeable odor, you can reuse the ones that came with your furniture. If you need new rolls, buy new ones of the same dimensions as the ones originally in your furniture. They can be obtained, ready-made, from a professional upholsterer; trying to stuff your own is cumbersome work, and not recommended for beginners.

When installing an edge roll, you either tack it to a wood edge, or sew it to a burlap-covered edgewire. To follow a sharp turn, you notch the edge roll's flange or butt two edge rolls together (see illustration 36). Round the more gradual curves by sharktoothing the edge roll's flange with a series of small notches.

If you're tacking your roll down, allow it to overhang the outer wood edge by ¼ inch, with its flange facing the area to be stuffed. Use #12 tacks for most

FORMING EDGE ROLL INTO A SHARP CURVE

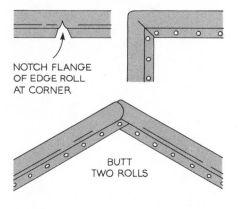

NOTCH FLANGE
OF EDGE ROLL
AT CORNER

BUTT
TWO ROLLS

FORMING EDGE ROLL INTO A GRADUAL CURVE

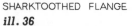

SHARKTOOTHED FLANGE

ill. 36

woods, and #8 tacks for hard woods. Drive tacks—2 inches apart—into the flange, angling the points slightly toward the burlap tube of the edge roll, as close to the tube's base as possible.

Step by step: Sewing an edge roll to a fully up-holstered armchair's edgewire

If you must sew your edge roll into place, the following guidelines will help you.

1 To begin stitching edge roll flange's rear to springs' burlap cover at chair's front, thread a 6-inch curved needle with a length of upholsterer's twine or heavy-duty polyester thread, twice the length of edge roll.

2 Face edge roll's flange toward springs, allowing tube

to overhang burlap-covered edgewire by ¼ inch.

3 At roll's end, in middle of edgewire's curve toward chair arm, plunge needle through flange and underlying burlap on edgewire's inside edge. Thrust needle under edgewire and out at edgewire's side, through the vertically draped burlap. Tie an upholsterer's slipknot (see page 100).

STITCHING EDGE ROLL FLANGE TO BURLAP

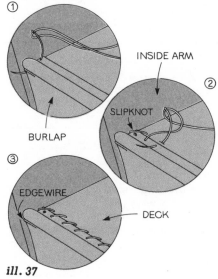

①

BURLAP

INSIDE ARM

②

SLIPKNOT

③

EDGEWIRE

DECK

ill. 37

4 Moving away from knot, one inch toward opposite end of edge roll, plunge needle through burlap covering chair's deck just behind flange of edge roll (don't catch a spring), back up through burlap under flange and through flange itself.

5 Continue to repeat Step 4 parallel to edgewire—you need not catch edgewire. Pull stitches tight so that edge roll doesn't move easily.

6 When you reach roll's opposite end at middle of edgewire's curve toward other chair arm, plunge needle through flange and burlap underneath. Thrust needle under edgewire and out at edgewire's side through vertically draped burlap. Secure thread with two half hitches.

7 The next step is to stitch edge roll tube's front to edgewire. Beginning again at end of roll where edgewire curves toward chair arm, plunge needle through tube's lower front on edgewire's inside edge. Thrust needle under edgewire, and out through vertically draped burlap. Tie an upholsterer's slipknot.

8 Moving away from knot, one inch toward opposite end of edgewire, plunge needle through tube's lower front on edgewire's inside edge. Thrust needle under edgewire, and out through vertically draped burlap. Loop thread from previous stitch around needle point as it emerges through burlap. This locks the stitch (see illustration 38).

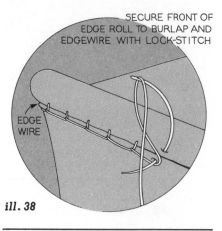

SECURE FRONT OF
EDGE ROLL TO BURLAP AND
EDGEWIRE WITH LOCK-STITCH

EDGE
WIRE

ill. 38

9 Continue to repeat Step 8 parallel to edgewire.

10 When you reach roll's opposite end, plunge needle through tube's front on edgewire's inside edge. Thrust needle under edgewire, and out through vertically draped burlap. Secure thread end with two half hitches.

11 If edge roll is able to bend over lip when someone sits on seat, padding can slip forward, out of place. Test your edge roll by pressing down on it. If it bends forward, stitch as in Steps 7 and 8, only bring needle through tube's lower rear and underlying deck burlap (instead of tube's front and vertically draped burlap) as you stitch along edge roll's length. Finish stitching as in Step 10, plunging needle through tube's rear.

Stuffings

Stuffings provide comfort when you sit down and lean back. They also soften your furniture's appearance.

Reuse or replace stuffing? Reuse the loose moss or hair stuffing in the shape you found it when stripping your furniture, if you can. If you're reusing cotton padding, fluff out any lumps and level hollows when you reapply it. No matter how you build back old stuffings, plan to flesh them out with a layer of new cotton to provide the smoothest possible underlayer for your outer cover.

Sometimes old stuffings smell or rot. Polyurethane foam can disintegrate. Or you may have found your furniture stuffed with inelastic excelsior wood shavings. What should you choose as replacement? Loose moss, horse or hog hair, and rubberized-hair stuffings give longest life and most resiliency. Because of its mesh back, rubberized hair is also easy to shape, using upholsterer's shears. Loose hair and moss are shaped by pushing or pulling into the desired conformation.

If you have trouble finding new moss and hair, polyurethane foam is a good substitute, and is

available at most fabric shops and foam supply houses (see "Shaping foam").

Covering foam with cotton padding in inside arms and inside backs minimizes its abrasion and decay. Hair or moss stuffings also must be covered with a layer of cotton padding. The better the quality of your cotton padding, the easier it is to mold and the less likely it is to fall apart when handled. Determine the cotton's quality by its whiteness and freedom from lumps. You may have more luck finding high-quality cotton padding at a professional upholsterer's than at a fabric shop.

How to stuff furniture. The theory of stuffing is this: place the coarsest, least expensive materials (such as organic fibers other than cotton or moss, if any such materials are used) next to the burlap or webbing foundation, stitching them in place (see sewing information under "Crowning,"

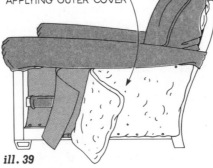

COTTON PADDING IS TACKED OVER OUTSIDE-ARM BURLAP JUST BEFORE APPLYING OUTER COVER

ill. 39

on page 110). Cover this first stuffing layer (if you have used one) with a layer of foam or hair, and cap that with a layer of cotton padding. If you are replacing the original stuffings with new ones, be sure to duplicate the original bulk and shape with the new materials, to insure that the furniture will be neither under nor overstuffed when you put its new cover on.

Two major exceptions to the theory of stuffing exist. The first is that hair, rubberized hair, moss, and polyurethane foam need no base layer of coarse stuffing. The second is that springless seats

(such as those possessed by pad-seated chairs) and any fully upholstered furniture's outside arms, outside back, back boxing, and front border require layers of cotton padding only—you add the new cotton just before applying the outer cover.

Shaping foam. Polyurethane foam is easy to shape. Purchase a foam slab from a fabric shop or upholstery supplier. Its dimensions should equal or exceed the dimensions of your original stuffing's greatest width, height, and length. Using a serrated bread knife or electric carving knife, pare the foam to match your original stuffing's shape and size. Pare only a little foam away at a stroke, so as to avoid cutting more off than you want. Compare the foam to your original stuffing frequently as you cut, to be sure you are replicating the original shape exactly. For maximum cutting ease, spray the knife's blade with silicone or a nonstick vegetable coating.

Step by step: Reusing deck and lip stuffing on a fully upholstered armchair

1 As a unit, hair side down, center old deck hair and cotton padding layers on top of deck's burlap surface. Align layers' straightest edge along future lip/decking seam, approximately four inches back from chair's front edge.

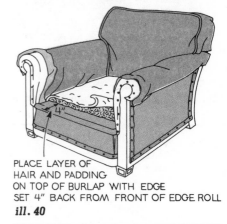

PLACE LAYER OF HAIR AND PADDING ON TOP OF BURLAP WITH EDGE SET 4" BACK FROM FRONT OF EDGE ROLL
ill. 40

2 With your palm, feel for hollows and lumps, especially at stuffing edges. If you find any, redistribute hair or add bits of new padding. Tuck in edges between deck and inside arms, and between deck and inside back.

3 Place lip hair or cotton (if no hair was used) so that back edge of it abuts deck stuffing at future lip/decking seam, and front edge overhangs edge roll by ¼ inch.

4 Cotton hugs lip and won't shift, but hair will shift unless sewn to burlap beneath. Thread 6-inch curved needle with upholsterer's twine or heavy-duty polyester thread. At one end of lip, plunge needle through hair, catch burlap, bring needle back up through hair, two inches toward other end of lip, and tie an upholsterer's slipknot (see page 100). Plunge needle again through hair and burlap, bringing it back up two inches away, and slipping it under previous stitch to lock it. Continue stitching in the same way across lip to opposite end. To secure last stitch, loop twine twice around emerging needle; pull twine taut.

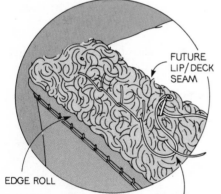

FUTURE LIP/DECK SEAM

EDGE ROLL

SECURE LIP HAIR TO BURLAP WITH LOCK-STITCH
ill. 41

5 Overhang lip hair (or cotton, if no hair was used) with a strip of cotton broad enough to cover hair and front of edge roll completely.

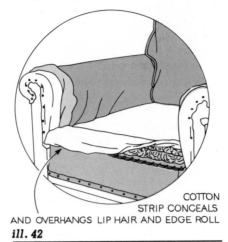

COTTON STRIP CONCEALS AND OVERHANGS LIP HAIR AND EDGE ROLL
ill. 42

6 Stuff cotton wads or hair salvaged from beneath arms between each side rail and arm liner.

Crowning. Tight seats and inside backs (those having no removable cushions), and padded arm tops, if stuffed with loose hair or moss, require crowning—building the stuffing's center higher than its perimeter. Crowning is necessary because the outer cover, when stretched tight for tacking, tends to press the stuffing out toward edges, depressing the center.

Start stuffing an area requiring crowning by building a small mound of loose stuffing in the middle of the section to be covered. Surround and top it, overlapping each successive layer little by little, so that the stuffing gradually extends outward toward the section's edges. You'll have to build up new, uncompressed hair or moss to a free-standing height two or three times the desired, compressed height before you can achieve adequate density. Check the density by applying pressure on the mounded stuffing with the palm of your hand. If you can feel wood, webbing, or springs, you'll need to add more stuffing. Used stuffing, compressed by long use, need only be rebuilt to the desired

height. Used or new, the last, top layer of stuffing should cover the entire section to be crowned.

To preserve a crown built over burlapped webbing or springs, sew the stuffing in a whorl pattern to the burlap with a straight 12 to 18-inch needle (a double-pointed needle is easiest to use) and upholsterer's twine or heavy-duty polyester thread.

SECURE STUFFING TO BURLAP USING 2" STITCHES IN A WHORL PATTERN
ill. 43

Start with a very short stitch secured by an upholsterer's slipknot (see page 100), catching a little stuffing in the knot to avoid forming a hard lump under the knot. Make 2-inch-long stitches over the stuffing, and ¾-inch-long stitches under the burlap. To secure last stitch, loop twine twice around emerging needle; pull twine taut.

To preserve a crown built over a solid base of wood, tack the stuffing to the base: make small openings in the fiber down to within ½ inch of the base at 2-inch intervals. Hammer a tack in each opening. Use #10 tacks.

GLOSSARY

Backing: Latexlike substance spread on upholstery fabric's wrong side to help keep the weave intact. Usually, the thicker the backing, the less expensive the fabric.

Backstitch: Stitching or a stitch in which the thread is doubled back on the preceding stitch(es). Eliminates the need to tie off a thread's end, and strengthens the seam end.

Barrelback: Chair or sofa with arms forming a continuous curve with its back.

Batting, quilted polyester: A kind of padding used to wrap springs or foam slabs before stuffing them into cushions.

Bias: A diagonal that intersects the crosswise and lengthwise threads of a piece of fabric.

Blind-stitch: To stitch together two fabric sections, their right sides facing each other, in such a way that the finished stitches are concealed.

Blind-tack: To tack or staple fabric on its wrong side and fold the fabric back over the tacks so they don't show.

Boxing: Fabric strip that links two larger pieces of fabric. For instance, cushion boxing links a cushion's top and bottom faces.

Cardboard strip, cardboard tacking strip: See Tacking strip.

Claw tool: Its bent shank and beveled, forked blade are designed to rid furniture of old tacks and staples.

Crowning: Building the center of a mound of stuffing higher than its perimeter.

Deck: Most of the platform that supports a loose seat cushion. Fabric covering the deck is called "decking."

Dustcatcher: Lightweight fabric tacked to the underside of an upholstered frame to prevent bits of upholstery material from dropping onto the floor.

Edge roll: Thick jute cord wrapped in burlap. Used to soften frame and spring edges.

Edgewire: Spring-based decks and backs are sometimes surrounded by this stiff, thick wire, to which outer springs are tied.

Foam, polyurethane: Less expensive and easier to handle than springs, polyurethane foam often fills cushions and replaces old hair or moss stuffings in seats and backs.

Frame: Basic structure of a sofa, chair, or stool. Usually made of wood or metal.

Front arm panels: Padded, upholstered wood panels used to cover arm fronts of some chairs and sofas.

Gimp: Ornamental braid used to cover tack heads that hold fabric's edge against exposed wood.

Hog ring: Heavy wire loop used to secure spring coils to webbing.

Illusory pleat: Backdrop of fabric that creates illusion of a skirt pleat when situated behind two skirt panels.

Lip: Front section of platform that supports a loose seat cushion. Has both a vertical and a horizontal face. See also Spring-edge lip.

Pile: Tiny, stand-up threads that form the surface of certain fabrics such as velvets and corduroys.

Railroaded: Describes fabric that runs horizontally along the width of a piece of furniture, and from front to back along its arms. See also Vertically run.

Repeat: Distance between centers of identical motifs, measured along the length of a bolt of fabric.

Selvage: Lengthwise border running along both edges of fabric, finished so as not to ravel.

Sharktooth: To cut small, closely spaced notches along a fabric section's edge, making it possible for the section to fit smoothly around a gradual curve.

Skirt: Fabric panel that sometimes surrounds the base of a piece of furniture and reaches to the floor, hiding the furniture's legs.

Slip-tack: To hammer a tack or shoot a staple only partially into a frame member so the tack or staple can be easily removed.

Spring-edge lip: Extended sofa or chair lip that's not attached to the furniture's arms. See also Lip.

Stretcher: Fabric scrap sewn to outer cover to extend cover into hidden areas of furniture, thus conserving expensive outer-cover fabric.

Stretcher tool: Spiked instrument that lets you pull strips of webbing taut before tacking them to seat rails.

Tacking strip: Cardboard strip, ½ inch wide, that gives a straight edge to a blind-tacked fold.

Tight seat or back: Fully upholstered seat or back designed not to have a cushion.

Top-stitch: To strengthen a seam by pressing seam allowances to one of the joined fabric sections, then sewing the allowances to that section with another seam, ¼ inch from the first.

Undercover: Fabric casing, usually muslin or burlap, that covers interior stuffing. Found mostly on older furniture, undercover is directly beneath outer cover.

Upholsterer's horses: Padded sawhorses that hold furniture off the floor so you can work without back strain.

Vertically run: Describes fabric that runs vertically, bottom to top, over furniture's front, back, and arms. See also Railroaded.

Webbing: Interwoven 3½-inch-wide jute strips that provide a foundation for many upholstered arms, backs, seats, and wings.

Webbing stretcher: See Stretcher tool.

Welt: Cord wrapped in fabric. Used to trim upholstery seams and places where fabric meets exposed wood. Single welt consists of one cord; double welt consists of two parallel cords.

INDEX